Sergeant Nicol

Sergeant Nicol

The Experiences of a Gordon Highlander
During the Napoleonic Wars in Egypt,
the Peninsula and France

Daniel Nicol

LEONAUR

Sergeant Nicol: The Experiences of a Gordon Highlander During the Napoleonic Wars in Egypt, the Peninsula and France
by Daniel Nicol

FIRST EDITION

Published by Leonaur Ltd

Text in this form copyright © 2007 Leonaur Ltd

Originally published in 1911 in the book
*With Napoleon at Waterloo and Other Unpublished Documents
of the Waterloo and Peninsular Campaigns*
edited by MacKenzie MacBride

ISBN: 978-1-84677-231-3 (hardcover)
ISBN: 978-1-84677-232-0 (softcover)

http://www.leonaur.com

Contents

Publisher's Note

This book, relating the first-hand experiences of Daniel Nicol in the Napoleonic Wars is important for several reasons. First, it is a significant Napoleonic memoir that offers details of historic events that were not recorded by any other memoirist of the period. Second, Nicol gives a rare account from the ranks of Moore's Egyptian Campaign, and finally, it gives one of the most detailed accounts available to us of what it was like to be a prisoner of war of the French during the time of Napoleon and Wellington.

We find it odd that Nicol's words have been overlooked for so long. Originally published in 1911 as part of the book *With Napoleon at Waterloo and Other Unpublished Documents of the Waterloo and Peninsular Campaigns* edited by MacKenzie MacBride, these three well written, witty and humane accounts surely deserve some permanence as a book in their own right? Although the material available to us was somewhat fragmentary, concentrating, as it does, on three episodes of Nicol's military career, we are pleased to offer the Leonaur book *Sergeant Nicol* to a wider audience.

The introduction that follows has been adapted by the Leonaur editors from MacKenzie MacBride's introduction to his book; 'About Daniel Nicol' has been used from Mac-

Bride's book without alteration. The sections 'With Abercrombie and Moore in Egypt' and 'A British Prisoner in France' have been altered only to address consistency of spelling and presentation, while 'Withthe Gordon Highlanders in Spain' retains some 'scene setting' comments by the editor of the original book (these have been set in smaller type with inset margins) before moving fully into Nicol's account which, again, has only been altered to address consistency of spelling and presentation.

The Leonaur Editors

Introduction

In the following pages Daniel Nicol, a soldier of the Gordon Highlanders, gives an account of his experiences as a Napoleonic era soldier in Egypt, the Peninsula—from where he relates vividly the doings of a company of his regiment which was left behind in Spain and served under Wellesley at the Passage of the Douro and at the battle of Talavera—and as a prisoner of the French. In addition to the fact of it being a singularly vivid human document, Nicol's words add much to our knowledge of several important events, and particularly the account of the 92nd company at the Passage of the Douro and Talavera, of which there is no other known account.

Besides their historical value these journals throw an interesting light on the character and education of the men who then formed the Highland regiments; for example, the following incident, related by Nicol when in Portugal:

About this time I was on picquet duty and was planted sentinel on a bridge over a river that runs in the valley, at daybreak I commenced to read a book, Butler's *Hudibras*, when in a moment a lusty friar made his appearance at the end of the bridge. This rather startled me, he saluted me, and was very friendly, looking at the frontispiece of my book, he exclaimed "Oh *Hudibras*! you are a *bon* Christian," and, pointing upwards and clapping me heartily on the shoulders, told me I was sure to go to Heaven. He gave me five *reas*, a copper coin of less value than a halfpenny, which I put in my pocket and carried for many a day as I did not wish to offend one who had so high an opinion of my being a Christian. But I had doubts of him, for a few minutes after, I saw him taking particular observation of a newly made battery on the road leading up to the heights.

Nicol, in fact, always seems to have had a book about him, though to-day it would astonish us to find a private soldier reading a book like *Hudibras*, but in those days education in Scotland was a solid thing. Further proof of this is afforded later where he tells how in the cathedral of Alcobace, the priests 'who offered great civility to our troops,' showed them two brass chains hanging from the roof from which they said two gold chandeliers had been carried away by the French. The parish schoolmaster had done his duty so well by Nicol that he was able to tell the priest, in the best Latin he could muster, which was so good that the Padre 'readily understood,' that he did not think the priests such fools as to allow gold or silver utensils to remain in their churches after they knew an enemy to be in their country.

At Coimbra the men visited the Royal Library in which the interpreter told them were books in every language in the universe. On this Sergeant MacBean, a sturdy old Highlander of the Gordons, began to speak in Gaelic to the professor and students who formed a ring round them. They were completely baffled, and afterwards MacBean made a boast that he had beaten the learned professors of the most learned town in Portugal. Nicol seems also to have been strongly possessed of the 'historic sense' as is shown in his remarks on entering Egypt.

We were now upon Scripture ground, we had come from a distant island of the sea to the country of the proud Pharaohs to carry on war where Nebuchadnezzar and Alexander the Great, Caesar and the other warriors had put armies in motion.

The soldier of the Napoleonic wars was badly paid, his pension when he got one at all was small, he suffered from all kinds of petty tyranny from officers often possessing half his own experience; and rain and frost and snow, hunger and thirst and weariness, were his familiar friends. Promotion from the ranks, though of everyday occurrence in the French army, was almost unknown in ours, and in reading these diaries one cannot but be impressed at the unfairness and the foolishness of a system which made it possible for men of the high stamp of Nicol to go unrewarded by a commission.

In view of all these things, and especially of the fact that, while honours were showered upon the officers which must have in many single instances cost the nation far more than the paltry rewards meted out to entire regiments of rank and file, one cannot help being impressed with the great debt we owe these intrepid soldiers of Egypt and the Peninsula, without whose steadiness and splendid instinct for giving to their leaders the best that was in them, Britain must inevitably have become a province attached to a great Napoleonic Empire.

MacKenzie MacBride

About Daniel Nicol

The soldier to whom we are indebted for the graphic details which follow was Daniel Nicol, a native of Crossford in Lanarkshire, his grandfather being tenant of the farm of Nemphlar under Lockhart of Lee. Young Nicol was caught by Lord Douglas's gamekeeper while poaching in the Clyde, and was to have been brought before the sheriff at Lanark. To avoid this exposure he made his way to Edinburgh and enlisted on the 12th March 1784, in the regiment of Highlanders then being raised by the Marquis of Huntly. He mentions that, after being taken to the Council Chambers and passed by a surgeon, he received a red jacket turned up with yellow facings, white trousers, and three ostrich feathers stuck in his hat.

It was not till he reached Aberdeen that he received his full uniform, a short jacket faced with yellow, a kilt and bonnet, in time for King George's birthday on the 4th June; and shortly afterwards the whole town was *en fete* when the news arrived of Lord Howe's great victory gained on the 1st June over the French fleet off Ushant. A treat was given to the soldiers in town, who paraded over the links 'where a bullock was roasted and twelve hogsheads of porter set abroach. Dancing and sports were kept up to a late hour, while the Freemasons, with the trades in town, walked in procession with their emblems, etc.' He adds: 'Some fine looking men were brought for our regiment by Captain Cameron of Fassifern, and on Tuesday, 24th June, the regiment was embodied by General Sir Hector Munro. The test of fitness set by the General was that each man should run past him for fifty paces, when only one man was rejected being too old.' The Gordons then numbered seven hundred and sixty men, of whom seven hundred and fifteen were Scottish, chiefly from the northern counties, many speaking only the Gaelic language; there were also thirty-two Scots-Irish, twelve English, and one was a Welshman.

Nicol saw service of a most interesting kind in the suppression of the rebellion in Ireland; and after engaging in the expedition to Holland, where he took part in the battle of Egmont op Zee, he passed through the whole campaign in Egypt from Aboukir to Cairo. After a spell of garrison-work in Ireland and in Glasgow, the corps was sent to Denmark and Sweden in 1807 and in the following year on its return to England, was despatched to Portugal.

With Abercrombie and
Moore in Egypt

CHAPTER 1

Captain Livingstone

We sailed on the 24th of June 1801 under sealed orders, leaving the ships of the Channel fleet behind us. We had a very quick and pleasant passage to the Straits of Gibraltar, where our ship ran foul of an American merchant vessel and damaged her much. Our commodore informed us that our destination was Minorca, there to join an expedition that was forming under our old friend Sir Ralph Abercrombie to assist the Austrians in Italy. We passed through the Straits but did not touch at Gibraltar and on the 17th July fell in with the *Bulldog* gun brig on her way home with despatches; they told us that Malta had surrendered.

We had very light winds off the coast of Spain in passing Yvica and Majorca, and arrived at Minorca on the 21st of July. We then learned that Sir Ralph Abercrombie and Lord Keith had been at Genoa and had offered to land 6000 troops, which offer had been refused by General Melas. On 14th June the battle of Marengo was fought, which sealed the fate of Italy and the French took possession of the country. Many of the inhabitants of Genoa were actually on the point of starvation and supplies of provisions were sent to them from the British fleet. Lord Keith arrived on the *Foudroyant,* 80, and Sir Ralph in the *Kent,* 74.

Disputes arose betwixt our officers and the captain of the ship about having the regiment inspected on deck. One day he bawled out, 'There is but one God in heaven, and only one commander on board his Majesty's ship *Diadem*; and I am he—Thomas Livingstone.' This his crew knew well, for he was a tyrant.

The regiment was ordered out to bathe and swim and a number of us swam ashore. I took my canteen and a comrade had a Spanish dollar so we sent for wine and were sitting on the beach enjoying ourselves when unfortunately General Foxe and his suite came riding past. He ordered us all to be taken to the main guard. In a moment we jumped into the sea and, by diving among some small vessels lying near the shore, got all clear off except Corporal John MacDonald of our company, who was caught by an aide-de-camp and taken naked as he was to the main guard. All the others got on board safely except myself who, having a canteen slung round my neck was nearly drowned when one of the ships' boats came to my aid. An oar was put under me and I was raised up and taken on board insensible. A shocking thing it would have been if I had been drowned in this condition, but the Lord has ever been merciful to me. Next morning the swimmers ashore were put in irons and we lay at the wardroom door for thee days. One of my comrades had secured my canteen full of wine, which had been searched for by the master at arms. On the third day all hands were piped up to see the swimmers flogged for going on shore without leave; but being all men of the very best character, it was decided that one should suffer for the whole. Lots were drawn and the lot fell on James Gardner, who took his punishment very contentedly.

Corporal MacDonald was tried by garrison court-martial, and our company having given most of the offenders was sent ashore to see the sentence carried out at the back of the quarantine island. This was a mess we had got into innocently enough; it was the first offence with most of us and nearly all the squad rose to be useful non-commissioned officers.

The troops were landed for refreshment and exercise and the vessels cleaned out. Our regiment landed at Georgetown where lay the 42nd and 90th regiments. Wine was very cheap here, about 3d. the bottle and rum and brandy sold for about 5d. the bottle, so many a gallon was drunk with our old acquaintances in these regiments whom we had not seen since we left the Rock. Bread was dear. On the 7th of August Colonel Erskine ordered us all to get sober as it was our turn to take duty to-morrow. I was made corporal on the I2th of August 1800, and mounted Little Bay guard at the back of the fort. Our regiment was inspected on the glacis by Sir Ralph and General Foxe and we were paid up on to the 24th of July. I got liberty to go to Port Marion, one of the chief towns in the island; it has some good streets and buildings. In the dockyard undergoing repairs was the French ship *Genereux*, eighty guns, taken while trying to escape at the battle of the Nile and the *Guillaume Tell*, taken at Malta. I returned to Georgetown by water on 30th March 1806. We got blue pantaloons and black gaiters served out. Lieutenants George Fraser and Gordon's wounds broke out afresh and both officers were sent back to England.

Minorca is of great service to Britain, it having a large harbour with water so deep that war vessels can come within a few feet of the shore. It is well sheltered by hill and there is plenty of fresh water which makes it very serviceable to our fleets in the Mediterranean; but now that Malta is in our possession it is not likely we will retain them both. The harbour is well defended by batteries on one side and by Fort St George formerly St Philip on the other. The chief town is Crudadella about 30 miles from Port Mahon; it is very strong, with batteries cut out of the solid rock and mounted with heavy guns; four regiments were doing duty here. The island has a barren appearance and most of the articles here are brought from other ports of the Mediterranean. The inhabitants appeared to me to be smaller than the generality of Spaniards.

We embarked on the 30th and sailed on the 31st. Colonel Erskine got the regiment transferred from the *Diadem* where we had been very uncomfortable to the *Stately*, 64, Captain Scott, who was quite a different character from Captain Livingstone; it was a pleasure to be on board his ship. We had very light winds and came close on the small island of Alberan, half-way between Spain and Barbary. On the 14th September we anchored in Tetuan Bay to the south east of Gibraltar belonging to Morocco. Here the fleet completed its stores of provisions and water and on the 29th sailed with a light breeze; passed the Spanish garrison of Ceuta on the north point of Africa opposite Gibraltar which is, I believe, very strong; some gunboats are stationed there ready to take an advantage when it offers. We thought we were to attack this place, so that we might command both sides of the straits. In this we were mistaken, but the garrison gave some of our vessels that came within range a salute of round shot, which our men of war were not slack in returning.

CHAPTER 2

Why the British Did Not
Take Cadiz

On Wednesday the first of October we anchored in Cadiz bay alongside our blockading fleet. On the 3rd the fleet and troops under command of Sir James Pulteney arrived. They had sailed from home in July and had attempted in August to cut out the Spanish fleet at Ferrol but did not accomplish it. They then put in at Vigo Bay where they lost the *Stag* frigate. They had just kept the enemy's coast in alarm, as we had been doing.

The *London*, 98, arrived and anchored close to us. Four days' provisions were served out on the 6th and we got sixty rounds of ammunition and everything was made ready for the landing which was to be near the town of St Mary's. The war vessels had taken up their position and the 1st division of the troops were in the boats and were moving off for the shore, when a flag of truce was sent out from Cadiz to the Admiral's ship. Some of our gun brigs were fired on by the batteries and we could see the Spanish troops running along the beach to oppose our landing. Meanwhile the flat-bottomed boats continued to move towards the shore when a gun was fired from the Admiral's ship and a signal hoisted for the boats to return and put the troops on board their respective ships. We were struck with the suddenness of the change, which was received with discontent by the whole army.

A report was spread that the place had been ransomed by money. Be that as it may some agreement was come to the terms of which will probably never be known to us. There was one thing however, and perhaps it was the only reason, that prevented our landing; Yellow fever was raging in Cadiz at the time. The troops were very anxious to land as they had been a long time afloat, and we thought that with an army of 30,000 and a large navy, we could easily have taken the place, especially as we had come unexpectedly upon them and they had few troops to make resistance. But doubtless our chiefs knew their orders and they also knew that it is a Briton's right to grumble.

Cadiz has a fine appearance from the sea studded with fine white houses round the bay to St Mary's. We left the bay of Cadiz on the 7th returning to Tetuan Bay and part of the fleet put into Gibraltar. We anchored in a semicircle, the war vessels outside the transports to prevent the Spanish gunboats from molesting them. One of them had tried to surprise one of our store ships in the night time but was chased under their own fortifications by our guard boats.

On the 15th the north-east wind rose to so great a height that our boats which had gone with empty casks to get water, were obliged to return to the ship and leave the casks, after being filled on shore, and the storm kept increasing as the night came on. There was much rain, lightning and thunder. All was bustle among the shipping. Our cable slipped and we began to drift; we then let go our best bower cable and anchor; the vessel caught fire by the cable running over the bitts and was only extinguished after great exertions by the seamen. We still kept dragging, so we were obliged to slip and put to sea. This was done at great risk, for we were in the midst of a large fleet, and were in danger of running foul of one or other of the ships. Although the night was very dark and the vessels were crashing against each other, yet by the goodness of God we steered clear and got up our staysails. All our boats were on board except a large flat-bottomed one which was dragging at our stern; in the morning nothing of it remained but the keel and the ring bolts by which it was fastened. On the 16th we were close on the coast of Spain and out of our large fleet saw only a store ship. We took her in tow with a hawser but were nearly pulling her under water so she had to throw off. In the afternoon we put right before the wind and made for Gibraltar; got round Europe Point and went down the bay under shelter of the Rock, thinking we were safe out of storm but, as we passed the *Foudroyant*, the Admiral ordered our Captain to lay about his ship and pass through the Straits round Cape Spartel to No. 7 on the west coast of Barbary, the rendezvous for all vessels leaving Tetuan. Our captain said that he had lost his anchors, was in want of provisions, etc. To this the Admiral replied, 'I don't care a d—; you must go where you are ordered.' At this we were not at all pleased, as it had the appearance of being a dismal night and I recollected the fate of the *Courageux* which was dashed to pieces while getting out of the bay.

We put about accordingly and passed through the Straits before the wind, going about eight miles an hour under bare poles. On the 17th it still blew very hard; we set the foretopsail and tried to bear up to No. 7 but it would not do. A gun got loose on the lower deck and cleared all before it and some men were hurt before it could be secured. Shortly after this the foretopmast yard broke and came down, the sails flying like ribbons; two seamen were hurt, one had his thighbone broken. We ran along the coast of Africa, keeping the land in sight and the weather becoming moderate we came to anchor about four miles from the shore off the town of Sallee. A boat was sent ashore with one of the lieutenants to inform the Governor, who sent us a bullock which was very acceptable as our rations of late had been flour and salt pork; the Governor got some gunpowder in exchange for his bullock.

On the 20th the wind changed and we steered back again and joined the fleet at the appointed place, got our damages repaired, and received an anchor from the *Ajax*; we then set sail and anchored in Tetuan Bay for the third time, on the 26th. The ships No. 7 arrived and our regiment sent a picquet ashore to the watering place which is situated very conveniently; deep water with a fine sandy bottom and plenty of good fresh water near the shore. The Moors claim a big-gun cartridge from every ship getting water. We formed a chain of sentries to keep them back, which was not easily done, for they crowded around us selling figs and grapes and other fruits. These natives were of a stout make but were poor and miserably clad. One of them ran off with a bayonet which he took from the muzzle of one of the sentries' muskets. Complaint was made to one of their *sultans* or officers. The man was pursued and brought back, laid on his back and *bastinadoed* on the soles of his feet with a pole about six feet long; he was afterwards carried away. This cleared the crowd and we had no more trouble with them. We got a supply of provisions, bullocks etc. from Tangier. This town I am told looks best at a distance. Their soldiers wear a long robe of coarse cloth of a dirty white colour, turbans on the head and sandals on the feet. They carry large clumsy firelocks and a cartouche box strapped round the waist. The country so far as I saw it had a wild uncultivated appearance.

On the 8th of November the fleet sailed in three divisions; the first two for Malta direct and the third, in which was the 92nd for Minorca, to get our provisions and stores completed. We reached that island on the 21st and found everything in a bustle with ships preparing for a long voyage. We now learned that we were bound for Egypt, to drive the French out of that country. Egypt was the word on every tongue; it had a novelty for us and we were all on the qui vive. Our ship was repainted, our rigging overhauled, and all our stores got in, which kept all hands at work. We escaped some very squally weather while lying here. Two Danish frigates came in from the Gulf of Venice sounding brass trumpets; these were the first armed vessels I saw of that nation.

We set sail again on the 27th, passed some high land belonging to Sardinia; came close to the Isle of Sicily at a place where the beach was gravely. In passing the small isle of Gozo to the west of Malta, one of the ship's boys while getting in a foretop studding sail, fell into the sea and was drowned. As Malta was a place of note on various accounts and amongst others as being the place where the apostle Paul suffered shipwreck, I did not quit the deck from the time we came in sight of it till we anchored in the harbour. The day was very fine with a steady breeze as we passed St Paul's Bay. We anchored on the 6th of December.

The entrance to the harbour is narrow; the water so deep that vessels can ride within a few feet of the shore; it opens out to the left towards the town of Cottaneo. On the Valetta side are storehouses for the shipping. Round this place batteries and cannon are placed in all directions, tier above tier, with forts etc., fit, if manned with stout hearts and willing hands to blow all the navies of Europe out of the water. In the middle of the harbour is the Grand Mason Lodge, a fort mounting four tiers of guns. The troops landed in brigades by turns, for air and exercise. Our regiment landed and marched to the glacis and formed there and had a full view of the defences of the town on the land side very strong, with walls, towers and trenches. We marched into the country about five miles and piled arms in some stubble fields, then walked about till evening when we returned by another road. We passed some fields of cotton; the bushes were about 3 feet high and some women were gathering what was ripe. The ground is rocky with very little soil to be seen and we were surprised to see gardens and vineyards where one would think scarcely anything could come to maturity, the ground being so dry and stony. The market is well supplied with fruits and garden stuffs from Sicily. We had to wait some time at the naval yard for boats to take us on board; the Maltese came among us selling wine, which is very cheap.

On the 20th a fleet arrived from home and brought our regiment about 200 volunteers, chiefly from the Caithness and Inverness Fencibles, with Lieutenant Brodie Grant and Ensign Baillie. They came in the *Resource*, 32, frigate. Some very strong regiments were left in Malta as they had been filled up from the militias, and their agreement was not to serve out of Europe, but the 9th regiment, 35th, 2nd battalion 36th, 2nd battalion 40th, 52nd, 2nd battalion 8 2nd, and the 40th flank companies, volunteered to serve anywhere.

We left Malta on the 21st and sailed for Marmorice Bay in Asia. We passed many of the Greek islands on our left about the Dardanelles entrance, on the way to Constantinople. Coasted along the south side of Candia the ancient Crete; the land lies low but rises high in the interior; it is inhabited chiefly by Greeks, who are subject to Turkey as are most of the islands in the Levant. Off the island of Rhodes we came up to Sir Sydney Smith's squadron which had come to meet us to be our guide on this coast. Our fleet lay to off the east end of Rhodes. The hospital ships were here with some of the medical staff to form a general hospital for the army. Rhodes has a fine fertile appearance from the sea with gardens and white houses but some of our men who were ashore told me that the walls and town were ruinous. Over the harbour which is now much choked up, once stood the famous Colossus, being a lighthouse in the figure of a man with a leg on each side of the entrance. This figure was regarded as one of the Seven Wonders of the World. The island was the residence of the Christian knights after their retreat from the Holy Land, and many sieges they stood and battles they fought before they were expelled from it. I felt a more than usual interest in looking at those places, from what I had read of them in history and Scripture; I stopped aloft on the foremast crosstrees until I could discern the objects no longer.

CHAPTER 3

A Turkish Governor

From Rhodes we stood direct for the mainland, Sir Sydney Smith in the *Nigre*, eighty gun-ship, leading the van, and entering a passage between two hills we wondered where we were going, for the inlet was very narrow and the ships ahead of us were going out of sight. When we got a little further we found a passage which turned round a very perpendicular hill as suddenly as if it had been the corner of a street. Into this passage we sailed and in a few minutes we were in one of the finest and largest bays, it is said, in the world. It is surrounded with hills except on the south-east side; these hills are covered with wood from the summit to the water edge. There are great numbers of wild beasts in the woods. On the east side of the bay stand the Turkish village and castle of Marmorice, in the province of Natolia, in Lesser Asia. Our Admiral saluted the castle with seventeen guns and the salute was returned. The war vessels anchored at the mouth of the bay. The Turkish Governor accompanied by Sir Sydney Smith, visited most of the ships. On coming on board the *Stately*, this long bearded Turk, who was between seventy and eighty years old, seeing some of our men on sentry on the gangway accosted them in Gaelic, which surprised them much. It turned out that he was a Scotchman from Argyleshire, of the name of Campbell and had been obliged to leave his country twenty years before for some misdemeanour. Some said it was he who had shot Lord Eglinton. Others held that he had killed a schoolfellow in a quarrel and fled the country to escape punishment. He had lost his nose in the late war between Russia and Turkey and had a silver one painted flesh colour. He dined on board with our officers and claimed relationship with Paymaster Campbell.

We pitched our tents on 2nd February 1801 on a pleasant plain by a little brook and our volunteers were landed from the *Resource* frigate. All the sick were likewise landed. Some vessels were despatched to Macri bay for bullocks and others to Smyrna and Aleppo for bread which was furnished us by the Turks, a kind of hard dried husk. We were glad to get this as we were then put on full rations and our biscuits were bad and full of worms; many of our men *could only eat them in the dark!*

A company of bakers arrived from England, hired at five shillings a day when at work and three shillings at other times with rations; these were the best paid men on the expedition. They erected a field bakery and the sick men were supplied with fresh bread. A market was erected on shore which was well supplied by the Greeks who came in boats from all parts of the Levant with the produce of their country.

On the 8th of February a storm came on from the southeast, with showers of hail or lumps of ice, the largest seen by any of us. The tents on shore were beaten down and riddled as if by musket balls. Trees were broken down and rooted up. When night came on it was dismal to hear the wild beasts yelling and howling in the woods; they came down to the plain so near that our sentries fired and killed some, though fires were kept burning in the rear of the tents to keep them at a proper distance.

Some sailors strayed from their party, stole a bullock and abused and struck the owners. They were detected bringing it on board. A complaint was made to the Admiral who had them tried by court-martial when two were sentenced to be hanged and the others condemned to be flogged. A gallows was erected in the market-place, the yellow flag hoisted on their ship, and the culprits sent ashore with halters round their necks. But the Governor and other Turkish officers begged their lives from Lord Keith, which were granted. We thought much of the Turks for this. The army was exercised by brigades in landing in flat bottomed boats, with regiments keeping in line and advancing or retreating on signals from the naval officers stationed in the boats. The men-of-war launches had field pieces fastened on the prow, with slides for the wheels; when the lashings were cut, the guns were run on to the beach ready to act with the troops: this was an excellent plan which we had felt the want of in Holland.

Parties were sent ashore from each ship to cut wood and many fine myrtle and box trees were felled for fuel, dragging the wood down the hillsides to the beach was fine exercise for us. Our regiment was employed for three days in the engineer department making fascines and palisades. We were frequently landed for exercise and were brigaded with the 1st Royal Scots and the 54th, under command of Sir Eyre Coote, a good man and brave soldier.

A French *polacre* from Marseilles on her way to Alexandria was captured and brought here; she was laden with brandy, hats, shoes, fans and trinkets for the French army.

An infectious slow fever broke out in our regiment. Few of us escaped it and those who were longest in catching the infection were the worst. Our condition on board the Stately contributed towards it for we had no hammocks or beds but only our camp blankets to sleep in. We lay on the under deck and when the weather was stormy so much water leaked in by the edges of the ports as made the lee side of the ship very wet. When she tacked, the water that was lying on the lee side would run across the whole deck and so we had to lie in the damp. This made us very uncomfortable and caused us to feel stiff and our bones sore. On this account our regiment was landed in Egypt very weak, when all its strength was needed.

Some vessels arrived from Britain with detachments for various regiments. Lord Keith was promoted from being Vice-Admiral of the Red to be Admiral of the Blue and Sir Richard Bickerton to be Vice-Admiral of the Red. A Turkish line of battleship, a frigate and some heavy gunboats arrived from Constantinople. One of their great men accompanied by Sir Sydney Smith was rowed round the fleet in a thirty oared barge, with a silk flag at the stern.

Arrangements being now complete, the troops were ordered on board, and the worst of the sick were sent to the General Hospital at Rhodes. The men of our regiment formerly on the *Resource* were put on board the *Niger*, 32, frigate, a clean vessel, the captain of which was a pious man and seldom was duty more pleasantly done than on board his ship. A number of Greek vessels were hired to carry horses and stores; and general orders were issued concerning our duty and our conduct towards the inhabitants of the country we were going to; we were especially cautioned not to interfere with them in the matter of their religion.

On Monday the 23rd of February the fleet weighed anchor and we were out of the bay before sunset. I took up my station with a few others on the foretop. As the fleet consisted of about 200 ships, many of which were large and elegant vessels, it had a grand and interesting appearance. The island of Rhodes lay on our right and the coast of Asia Minor on our left; and to see the last golden beams of the sun glancing on the wide spreading white sails with the wind beginning to blow fresh, brought to my mind what has happened on this very coast, of people being driven from their country going to found a new settlement under some adventurous chief. Little did I think while reading of these countries when a boy, that I should one day see them or that I should do the duty of a soldier on these coasts.

A Motley Crowd

The nations on board our fleet were many, Turks, Greeks, Albanians, Scotch, English, Irish, Corsicans, Maltese and a brigade of soldiers in our service composed of men from various parts of Germany. The wind got rather high and the Turkish and Greek vessels left us and took shelter in the nearest ports, although the weather was not what any British seaman would call bad, only squally. Their departure was a serious loss to the army for we were in want of the horses on board of them.

On the 26th we passed the island of Cyprus on the right; what we saw of it lay low, with trees to the water's edge. On the 28th we fell in with our squadron that was blockading Alexandria and on the 1st of March saw the low sandy beach of Egypt between Damietta and Aboukir bay, which is formed by the main branch of the river Nile, that flows past the town of Rossetta and forms the main entrance to the lakes.

We anchored in Aboukir bay on the 2nd of March. The night before the wind freshened and there were some heavy showers of rain. This made us remark that if there was no rain in Egypt there was rain very near it, contrary to the account given by the Bible; but this conversation was dropped on one observing that the Bible did not say that there never was any rain in Egypt but that when it spoke of there being no rain there, it meant that the land did not depend upon rain like other countries for raising the crops, but on the annual inundations of the Nile. We all agreed after we had marched through the country that the Scripture account of it was perfectly correct; and the universal remark was that a remnant of the plagues of Moses still existed in it.

Some of our men began to complain of the want of their ordinary sight. The wind continued high and the sea stormy and rough and any of our vessels getting near the shore were fired upon from the enemy's works; the shore seemed to be well fortified from Alexandria to the entrance of the lakes. A boat set off to reconnoitre on 28th February with General Moore and an Engineer officer. The French allowed it to come close in, but the instant it began to return a well aimed shot from the castle killed Lieutenant-Colonel MacKerris of the Engineers and wounded some others. So the French drew the first blood. Some guns were fired from a low sandy island at the mouth of the bay, (where the *Culloden*, 74, ran ashore in Nelson's engagement) this forced some of our ships to change their position. The *Foudroyant* fished up an anchor of the *L'Orient*, the French Admiral's ship that blew up at the battle of the Nile.

On the 7th the wind moderated and our gun brigs, cutters, and the Turkish gunboats, anchored as near the shore as they could, the water being very shallow; these with the armed launches were to clear the beach while the troops made good their landing in Egypt.

CHAPTER 4

A Hard Fought Landing

The troops first to land in Egypt were about 5,500, called the Reserve, under command of Generals Moore, Ludlow and Coote; the boats were under the conduct of Sir Sidney Smith, Captains Cochrane and Stephenson, R.N. These troops were in the boats by daybreak and at three o'clock were ordered to row for their rendezvous in rear of the light-armed vessels which were to protect the landing. This was a very fatiguing duty for the seamen, for the fleet was so widely anchored, and the large vessels so far from the shore, that it was nearly nine o'clock before the boats were collected and arranged.

The enemy could see all our movements and the delays which took place gave them a fair opportunity to collect their forces and provide for their defence, for they knew the only point at which we could land. Several regiments were put on board light vessels which went as near the shore as they could, that support might be quickly given on the return of the boats to those who landed first. Our regiment was in the 2nd division and we were spectators of the 1st's landing; and though we felt thankful we were not in the boats, yet our anxiety for those that were was as painful, I believe, as if we had been in them.

At nine o'clock the signal was given for the boats to advance and the whole line advanced very regularly, giving three loud cheers. The French were posted on the top of the sandhills, forming the concave of a circle of about a mile, 60 yards in the centre of which was a very steep height; their left extended to the blockhouse at the entrance to lake Maadie. To the right the shore was flat and covered with thick bushes, such as form the date or palm tree, which were favourable for concealing the enemy; while on the extreme right stood the castle of Aboukir which commanded the whole shore.

As soon as the boats set out for the beach, our bomb ketches and war vessels began to throw their shot and shells upon the shore, and the light vessels with their carronades, moving in a line with the boats began to fire. The enemy had twelve pieces of artillery on the heights and the beach and heavy guns on the tower in Aboukir castle. As soon as the boats got within reach of their shot they opened fire on them. The scene now became dreadful, the vessels pouring whole broadsides, the bomb ketches throwing shells and the gun-boats and cutters exerting themselves to the utmost. All eyes were directed towards the boats and every flash of the enemy's guns was noticed to see whether the shot struck the water or the boats, and when there was any confusion among them we wondered how many might be killed or wounded. But still the boats pressed on towards the shore and persevered in keeping good order. The firing from our war vessels over their heads did not for a moment interrupt the enemy's fire or silence a single gun.

We soon observed the right flank of the boats get nigh the shore, while the enemy from their elevated position began to pour volleys of musketry among them, our brave tars and soldiers giving them cheers for their shot and shell. In a few seconds after the 40th flank companies and the 23rd regiment were in line and without firing a shot cleared all that opposed them at the point of the bayonet, pushing them over the heights. This movement was clearly seen by all the fleet. The 42nd regiment was next seen ascending the heights; they charged the enemy opposed to them, who fled and disappeared. The left of the boats was the last to reach the shore, and the troops there were roughly handled before they got formed, and sustained a charge of cavalry; but they maintained their ground and in less than half an hour nothing was to be seen from the ships but the empty boats coming back for the 2nd division. Some of them soon reached the ship I was in and we lost no time in getting to the shore. On the way we saw some boats that had been struck with grape shot and swamped; the men in them had been picked up by the small boats in the rear which followed for that purpose.

We reached the shore in peace and quietness. The beach was strewed with dead and wounded men, and horses and cannon taken from the enemy. We formed in a hollow to the left of the centre height where many of the 42nd lay dead and wounded, and then advanced through the first range of sandhills and found the 1st division formed with their artillery which had been landed with them and were drawn by seamen. Our bringing our guns on shore along with the troops was what the enemy did not expect and it contributed much to their speedy retreat.

Eight pieces of cannon were taken from the enemy; their loss of men we could not learn exactly. Our loss was great, as was to be expected in front of an enemy posted to so much advantage; it was between 700 and 800 men of all ranks, the greater part of whom were killed or wounded in the boats previous to the landing.

We took up a position with our right to the sea and our left to the lake. Strong picquets were sent to the front, and we had likewise to watch the castle in the rear, which kept firing at anything that came near. Our first care was to learn whether water could be obtained in this sandy desert, and we were glad to find it could be got in the hollows by digging with our bayonets in the sand about 3 feet below the surface. All the troops were landed in the course of the day and the wounded were sent on board the fleet.

On the 9th, our regiment with a party of Corsican riflemen advanced along the peninsula to a place where it was contracted to about half a mile broad. The enemy had a redoubt here and a flagstaff for communicating signals between Aboukir Castle and Alexandria. We thought a stand would have been made here as the position was a good one; but the enemy had left it and thrown a large gun into the ditch.

In the course of the day the 42nd regiment relieved us and we went back to our former position, where we remained till the morning of the 12th. We made ourselves booths of the branches of the date tree to shelter us from the heavy dew which fell at night, and we had some showers of hail and rain which made it cold after sundown. Many of our men complained of blindness after sunset; this continued for days after we landed. By this time our ammunition and stores had been brought ashore and then began the landing of guns and the making of batteries and entrenchments across the neck of land so that we might attack the castle. This business was chiefly left to the naval officers and seamen of the fleet. The army got out three days' provisions and all was ready for a movement to the front.

But I must here give an account as well as I can of the troops landed; they were as follows: The first Division consisted of the 1st Royals, 2nd regiment, 8th, 13th, 18th, 30th, 44th, 50th, 54th (two battalions), 79th, 80th, 90th, 92nd, the Guards, De Rolle's regiment, Minorcans, Dillon's regiment. The Reserve consisted of the 23rd, 28th, 40th flank companies, 42nd, 58th regiments, a troop of Dragoons ditto of Hompesch regiment, the Corsican Rangers, and 12th and 26th Light Dragoons. About 300 seamen were landed with the guns as also a battalion of Marines.

The total force landed was about 15,000 men commanded by the following general officers: Hutchinson, Hope, Ludlow, Coote, Craddock, Stuart, Doyle, the Earl of Cavan, Moore, Oakes, Finch, Colonel Spencer, etc. The Engineers and Artillery were under Brigadier Lawson, Physician-General Dr Young, Sir Ralph Abercrombie, Commander-in-chief.

CHAPTER 5

The Gallant Stand of the 90th at Mandorah

On the 12th we advanced after filling our canteens with water; for in this dry sand, with a burning sun overhead and living on salt provisions, water is a precious article indeed. Having proceeded a little beyond the narrow neck of the peninsula the enemy's cavalry began to dispute the ground with us. Our march was slow and often interrupted; the ground being uneven and the sand very deep, parties were frequently sent to assist the seamen with the guns. Before night, we came in sight of the French army posted on a height. Their strength was about 6000, with cavalry, and from 20 to 30 field pieces. We halted and began to dig for water, which was greatly in demand; each company dug a well and we were out of patience till the water made its appearance but before we were half satisfied the regiment was ordered to picquet in front of the army. There was no help for it. We formed a chain of sentries; a half blind man and one that could see were put together; those that were quite blind were left in groups here and there in rear of their companies.

On the morning of the 13th our regiment formed the advanced guard on the left, and the 90th on the right. We got a little rum served out and began our march, leaving our knapsacks with a guard. Before we had gone far our light company which was in front fell in with the enemy's picquets and a skirmishing began. The light company was reinforced several times and drove in the enemy's outposts. The ground over which we marched was covered with thick bushes until we approached a rising ground on which the French were drawn up in order of battle. Our regiment kept to the side of the lake, the 90th was on our right, and the army followed us in two lines. The armed boats from the fleet had kept pace on the lake with the left of the army, but the water was now so shallow they could proceed with us no farther. We had a nine pounder field piece and a howitzer along with us; but very little ammunition for them.

As soon as the 90th had cleared the broken ground and began to ascend the height, a heavy body of cavalry advanced to charge them. The 90th formed in line, but before their line could get formed on the left the cavalry was close on them. We thought it was all over with the 90th but they stood firm, and when the cavalry were about to strike at them they opened their fire; it ran from right to left like a rattling peal of thunder. By this well-timed volley they saved themselves most gallantly, and the cavalry being so near, not more than 20 yards distant, it proved most destructive to them. Of those that wheeled past the left of the 90th few returned, and many horses were seen galloping with empty saddles.

During this transaction which was all over in a few seconds, our regiment made a pause, but on the retreat of the cavalry we again advanced. The enemy then began to open their artillery upon us from the heights but we still pressed on and they, seeing we were considerably in front of the army, formed the resolution of cutting us off before we could obtain assistance from the main body. When we saw their intention we halted, formed five companies in line and extended the other companies in rear of the bushes on the left towards the lake. We kept at them with our two guns until the last shot of ammunition was fired when they were drawn off to the rear.

Our situation was one of great danger. The enemy in front was advancing in a line formed like the blade of a scythe, the curved point towards the lake and that part was cavalry, said to be the dromedary corps. It seemed as if they meant to turn our left and get into our rear, while they attacked us in front, and, getting round our right, they would thus have surrounded us and made us prisoners or have destroyed us at once as we were not above 500 strong and every minute were getting fewer. The enemy had some fieldpieces in front which were making sad havoc among us, every shot sweeping down some of our men. Our commanding officer ordered us not to fire but to stand firm until we could see their feet as they advanced from the hollow in front of us. When the order to fire was given, like magic it dispelled the gloom from our countenances and everyone did his duty manfully. We encouraged one another, firing and at the same time praying, for soldiers do pray and that very fervently on occasions of this kind and, I believe, serious thoughts were with most of us, even the most profligate.

Our first fire caused the enemy in front of us to halt; and they kept firing on us; this we were not slow in returning, the smoke soon making us almost invisible to each other.

Our men on the left posted among the bushes did their duty admirably and maintained their ground. But our ranks were getting very thin in this unequal combat. To our great joy a party of the Marine battalion doing duty on shore arrived on our right and Dillon's regiment on our left. On the first fire of these troops the enemy retreated in a hurry.

We pursued them to some distance and Dillon's regiment coming up with a party of them charged and took two pieces of cannon. The enemy was so closely pressed that he divided his forces; part of them retreated through a shallow part of the canal and the other part retired upon Alexandria. Had our cavalry been mounted and we had ammunition for our few guns we would certainly have taken all the enemy's artillery and Alexandria into the bargain, for we were nearer to it than that part of the enemy's force which retreated to the left. The 90th lost about 400 and the 92nd about 200 in this action.

Our army formed in line on the heights the French had occupied in the morning. They kept cannonading us through the day and annoyed us much with their sharpshooters as we kept shifting about taking up different positions, making room for the troops coming up from the rear. This day was very warm and we suffered much from thirst; I have seen a Spanish dollar offered for a draught of water and in some instances refused.

The enemy now concentrated his forces on the heights of Alexandria. Our division advanced to possess the high ground on the left in rear of the canal over which was a bridge defended by a party of cavalry and infantry with two guns which played upon us as we formed in close column of companies ready to descend into the hollow. The 44th regiment was sent to the front and at the point of the bayonet captured the bridge; the party which defended it retired into their own lines. The enemy then began to move some heavy columns on the plain and opened on us with his artillery, thinking I suppose, to draw us under the guns of his fortifications; but our troops were ordered to screen them-selves by the heights. Those who had no shelter sat or lay down on the ground so as not to be so much exposed to the enemy's shot, but still were ready to be up and at them if they offered to come nearer. Our regiment retired to the rear and sent out parties in search of water, which had been in great demand during the early part of the day. They were fortunate in finding it; and the eagerness with which each man grasped his canteen and the pleasure it gave can only be imagined by those who have been in similar circumstances. We remained in the same position till near sunset, the enemy still cannonading us and cutting down a file here and there. Major Napier had a narrow escape from one of these shots.

By sunset the enemy took up the position in which it remained during the siege of Alexandria; our right to the sea and our left to the canal that separates Lake Maadie from the bed of the Lake Mareotis. We soldiers thought we had nothing to do but take the town whenever our heavy battering guns and ammunition arrived: but alas, much had to be done before the surrender of Alexandria.

As soon as our position was adjusted and we had piled arms, the cry was for more water and parties were sent out who brought it to us as thick as puddle, as men and horses had been promiscuously knee-deep amongst it trying, as it were, who could drink the fastest. After getting our water, being much fatigued we sat down among the sand and began to examine our haversacks. I observed some holes in mine; and taking out some biscuits found a grape shot in the centre of a bit of pork. I might well return thanks to God for the protection afforded me this day. Many miraculous escapes some of my comrades made; but our loss was great. Colonel Erskine was severely wounded in the thigh by grape shot; Captain Ramsay, Archibald MacDonald, Cameron and Palton wounded; Lieutenants Norman MacLeod, Ranald MacDonald and Donald MacDonald, C. Dowse, Tomline Campbell, Alexander Cameron and

Foreman wounded; Ensign Wilkie wounded; John Mackintosh, sergeant-major wounded in the right arm. In all our regiment lost about 150 in killed and wounded; but our wonder was how so many had escaped. The loss sustained by the army was about 1,500 in killed and wounded of all ranks. Four field pieces were taken from the enemy; their loss otherwise I never learned.

Colonel Erskine was taken on board one of the ships of the fleet when, after having one of his legs amputated he died on the 23rd. His remains with those of some other officers who had died on board were buried in the sand in front of the regiment. Lieutenant Dowie died on the 16th and Norman MacLeod about a month after. Tomline Campbell died on the 17th May.

On the 14th the commander-in-chief in general orders bestowed great praise on the 90th, 92nd, and Dillon's regiment for the bravery and steady conduct manifested by them while on the advanced guard yesterday; for maintaining their ground against a superior force of the enemy and baffling the enemy's attack until the line was closed up and formed. This day parties were sent to bury the dead and assist the wounded to the boats. I buried John Nicol from Banff, the only namesake I had in the regiment. He had been struck in the centre of the body by a large shot which had doubled him up; he lay a shocking sight, but his death must have been in a moment.

We got our tents on shore and pitched and were employed in landing heavy guns which had to be dragged to the heights through the sand. The fatigues of the army were very great, building batteries, raising redoubts and making entrenchments; the men affected with night blindness had to take their turn of night duty. The sentries on the outposts were all doubled, a blind man and a seeing man were put together, the former to hearken and the other to look out; and a blind man and one that could see were set to work together, to carry two handed baskets filled with earth to raise the breast works, the one that had sight leading the blind. Every place that could be fortified from the sea to the lake was made as strong as it could be in so short a time. On the large central height was what might be called our Grand Battery where proudly floated the British flag. From this place we had a view of all the plain to the fortifications of Alexandria.

When the working parties were digging among the ruins and turning up fine pillars and blocks of marble and placing in the breastworks and redoubts these ornaments of ancient palaces, it made me and many others reflect on the ancient glory of Egypt of which there are so many evidences even in the barren peninsula of Aboukir. I saw in these ruins the fulfilment of Scripture and from the description which I read on board ship after I knew we were bound for this place, I supposed such a city might have stood in this vicinity.

These reflections gave great interest to our operations. We were now upon Scripture ground; we had come from a distant island of the sea to the country of the proud Pharaohs to carry on war where Nebuchadnezzar and Alexander the Great, Caesar, and other great warriors had put armies in motion.

Our camp stretched from the sea to the lake on which were numerous boats bringing provisions and military stores from the fleet, while parties of seamen and soldiers were dragging them through the deep sand from the depot about two miles in rear of the army. This fatiguing work was cheerfully done notwithstanding the hardship that attended it. On the 17th Colonel Bryce of the Guards while visiting the picquets at night got among the French outposts; he was wounded and taken prisoner; he died a short time after. On the 18th our cavalry on the plain disputed a round hill with some French cavalry and on charging the French were fired upon by some infantry posted in rear of the hill; on this our cavalry turned and took some prisoners.

CHAPTER 6

The Night Attack At Alexandria

About 400 of our men were left on board the fleet ill of
fever when we landed; on the 20th our regiment being so
much reduced, having scarcely 300 fit for duty; was ordered
to march next morning to Aboukir to do duty there until
our strength was recruited. We marched long before daybreak, and left our tents standing for a regiment that was to
come from the second line to take our place. We had gone
but two miles on our road, when we heard the discharge of
musketry on our left. On this we halted and immediately
could see more firing, even the flash of every pan was vis-
ible from where we stood; then we heard a fieldpiece and
after that a roar of musketry. We knew there was a strong
guard with the working party about that spot, and that a
gun was with them. As the firing ceased we thought it was
a false alarm and began to proceed on our journey but
had not gone many steps when we heard the discharge of
some muskets on the right of the army. This produced a
voluntary halt with out any word of command. Some more
discharges were heard in the same direction. We were then
ordered to the right about and we went as quickly as possible to the tent of the commander-in-chief. By this time
the firing on the right was going on briskly among the

picquets. We were now ordered to take up the position we had left. It being still very dark our artillery began to play with the help of lighted lanterns, to let the men see to load. By the time we got to our position the action was close and heavy on the right of the line, and in the darkness not one regiment knew what the others were doing, or what was opposed to them, so they had to stand in awful suspense till the firing came in front of them. There could be no doubt of a powerful and determined attack by the enemy.

When we arrived at our post we found the ground unoccupied, the regiment which was to take our place not having arrived. This would have been a fine passage for the enemy to have entered had they only known of it; and we just arrived in the very nick of time when the enemy had gained the brow of the hill in our front, and a column was advancing towards the opening in the line where we should have been. We filled up the opening and fired on the enemy's column whenever we came up. And if this column had resolutely pushed forward, it might have done great mischief in the rear before it could have been overpowered; but on receiving our fire it retreated under the brow of the hill out of our sight, but left a line of sharp-shooters which annoyed us very much. Thank God, daylight began to appear and we could see what we were doing and where the danger was, as before this the only order that could be given was: 'Stand fast, and defend yourselves to the last, if attacked.' At this time the battle was raging on the right with terrible fury, and the brigade of Guards next to us on the right was closely engaged. The roar of the artillery was dreadful, and little could be seen through the smoke but the red flashes.

The action was short and severe and great injury was sustained by the right wing of our army, while the left was only partially engaged. The object of the enemy was to dislodge our troops on the right and then drive the army into the lake. He expected to gain the heights before daybreak and being well acquainted with the ground and the way we were posted, he could easily attack us in the dark. But we were not to be taken by surprise, as it was our practice to stand under arms an hour before daybreak. So instead of the enemy driving us into the lake, we drove them back out of our lines into the plain with great loss. Here they formed into columns, and a shell, the last one that did execution, was fired from the flagstaff battery, which fell in the centre of their columns and blew up an ammunition wagon and made a great scatter among them. About eleven o'clock the enemy retired under the protection of their own batteries.

General Menou, the French commander-in-chief, who had posted from Cairo to drive us into the sea, and who said that it was only Turks who had landed and that he did not believe a British army was in Egypt, found out this morning that his old stubborn enemy had landed, and was not to be chased or drowned at his pleasure. It was reported that a copy of his orders was found in the pocket of General Roiz who was killed in our lines, that no quarter was to be given but that we were all to be put to the sword or driven into Lake Maadie. The plan of attack was first to draw our attention to the left, while the coup de main was to be on the right, by the hollow between the flagstaff and the ruins of Ptolemy's palace, where the 28th regiment was posted and where it did good service. The French fought desperately and got among the tents of our first line, their cavalry charging through the hollow was stoutly opposed by the 42nd, which suffered severely, as did also the right wing of the guards; the foreign brigade from the second line was sent to their assistance under General Stewart. About this time and place our worthy commander-in-chief, Sir Ralph Abercrombie, was mortally wounded; he died on the 28th, and was deeply regretted by the whole army; General Moore was again wounded.

Our army by its losses in former actions, by parties absent at Aboukir on duty, and by sickness, had been reduced to about 10,000 before this action commenced, with about 40 pieces of cannon. The enemy's force was about the same number with the addition of cavalry. When he retreated he left 1,700 men dead and wounded on the field of whom above 1,000 were buried the first two days; he lost also 400 horses. Including the wounded who made their escape or had been removed, the enemy had lost one-third of the number he brought into action. The total loss of the British was about 1,500. The loss of our regiment was 50 men, Captain John Cameron and Lieutenant MacPherson wounded. We were now a small regiment indeed. This day I had a friend wounded in the left ankle; the wound never thoroughly healed. He was a pious lad, a very rare character indeed in the army in those days, and was a spiritual guide to me and many others. He was invalided and got a small pension; he now resides in Glasgow where he has been an example of goodness and uprightness. He has corresponded with me ever since.

Among those wounded was Corporal MacKinnon whom we thought to be dead when Sergeant MacLean saw some signs of life just in time to save him from being buried alive.

The result of this day was that we kept our ground and as a trophy took one of the *Invincible* standards belonging to the *32 demi-brigade*. It was lettered in the centre in gold PASSAGE DE SERVIA, PONT DE LODI, DE PAVIA, ET CASTEL NUOVO, etc., on a blue ground with laurels fringed with white. This flag was said to have been taken by Sergeant Sinclair of the 42nd, but got into the possession of Anthony Lutz of the Minorcan regiment after Sinclair was wounded. An investigation was ordered: Lutz got 20 dollars and a medal and a pension for life and Sinclair got a commission some time after. The standard after being exhibited to the army was sent to Sir Ralph, then lying on board the *Foudroyant*.

On the 23rd our regiment marched and reached Aboukir about nine in the morning before the day got excessively hot; we encamped beside a good well of water, the first I have seen in this country. Things were in a very different state from what they were when we were last here; then there was nothing but blood and carnage along the beach and the French Artillery from the top of the castle dealt death and destruction among us. Our people here had not been idle. Entrenchments and batteries had been made and the castle bombarded till the central tower was in a tottering condition and it was ready to fall before the enemy surrendered; 300 were sent prisoners on board the fleet. Marquees were pitched for the sick and wounded who were brought ashore. Many of the sick belonging to our regiment were put under the charge of Dr Hamilton, our own regimental surgeon, Dr William Findlay, being promoted to be physician to the forces.

A market was formed at the commissary's near the block house and the produce of the country was brought in by the Arabs who found a ready-money market for their goods, sheep, fish, vegetables and fruits; sometimes a kind of brandy was brought in in boats by the Greeks; but woe betide them if caught by the Turks selling liquor; they were at once seized and bastinadoed on the spot and their goods taken from them.

Alexander MacKinnon, a native of Arisaig and the author of several pieces of Gaelic poetry. His descriptions of the battles of Egmont and Alexandria are considered by those competent to judge as among the most spirited of modern Gaelic poems.

On my first visit to the market I bought a sheep for a Spanish dollar and a cheese about 10lbs. for 60 *paras* and a bunch of young onions. This was the first fresh provisions our mess had in Egypt and we could obtain for 3 *paras* as much fine bread as a man could eat. As the produce of the country was so plentiful our salt beef and pork were not used, but the casks stood at the quartermaster's for any one to take what he pleased, and it was no uncommon thing to see one piece of pork cut up to boil another with some green date branches, the only fuel we could get. This was extravagant enough. Our salt provisions ran up in the hands of the commissary to the value of 150, this sum was proposed to be given to the widows and orphans of the regiment.

The French barracks called the *Hutts* erected by them for their troops stationed at Aboukir, were converted into a general hospital; and at this place that dreadful calamity the plague first made its appearance. I was sent with a party there and we buried a surgeon and two women in one hole in the sand and seven men in another; all had fallen victims to it.

The wounded men seemed to be comfortable in the *Hutts* but were much tormented with flies and other vermin. I visited the castle which had annoyed us so much in landing, it surrendered on March 17th after a siege of five days. It stands on the point of the bay about 13 miles from Alexandria. Our dismounted dragoons were doing duty here. There is a ditch and drawbridge on the landside and it is nearly surrounded by the sea. The ramparts are mounted with mortars and cannon. In the centre stands the great tower on the top of which are two brass 32-pounders but the place is sorely battered by our shot and is in a tumble down condition. The view from the top of the tower is excellent; the east as far as the eye can reach is low and sandy, with date or palm trees which have a fine appearance at a distance; on the west stands Alexandria, which has a formidable appearance, with its towers and newly-raised fortifications; closer to us is a large plain, where the Turkish army landed and was defeated by the French. Many bodies lie here unburied and uncorrupted: the hot sun has dried all the moisture out of them and their skin was quite fresh like parchment. Near the castle once stood the town of Aboukir, now deserted and in ruins. This place had been under cultivation at some time, for we could trace where gardens had been and saw the remains of a few stunted fig trees, vines, etc. John Key of our company and Richardson of the 6th company were severely punished for going straight on to Aboukir on the morning of the 21st March when the regiment returned to the lines and giving the alarm that the French were driving us before them, and so causing great consternation among the sick and wounded.

A Turkish fleet sailed into the bay, and landed about 5,000 troops, 3 regiments of which had got British arms and accoutrements. They wore scarlet jackets, wide blue trousers tucked in at the knees, turbans and sandals on their feet; they had a number of flags of different colours. They were stout men, chiefly Albanians. These were the finest and best disciplined troops I had seen belonging to the Turkish army. April 2nd at twelve o'clock all the troops were under arms to receive the Turkish commander. He rode along the line with Lord Hutchinson. The Turkish flag was hoisted alongside the British on the castle.

The Hompesch cavalry, commanding officer Sir Robert Wilson, was sent here and dismounted, on account of some of them deserting to the enemy; their horses were given to the 12th Light Dragoons.

It was reported that a French fleet under Admiral Ganteaume was at sea on its way to relieve Alexandria. On this the seamen and the battalion of Marines were sent on board and Admiral Keith sailed in search of the enemy.

On the 13th of April openings were made in the banks of the canal leading from the Nile to Alexandria; and the water from Lake Maadie rushed into the bed of Lake Mareotis, which was nearly dry and passable in many parts both for horse and foot. The water continued to flow for about a month, having at first a fall of above 6 feet, when it nearly found its level; but there continued always a fall of above a foot owing to the sand absorbing the water. By this means a large extent of country was inundated. This contracted our position in front and protected our left from assault and armed boats and large germs could come up to the left of the line with stores and provisions.

With the strong batteries and entrenchments our men had raised since the action of the 21st March the army was secure, and Lord Hutchinson who had succeeded Sir Ralph Abercrombie as commander-in-chief, had a disposable force to march to the banks of the Nile while General Coote was left with the remainder to blockade Alexandria. Before this some of our troops had marched from the lines and with about 4,000 Turks had driven the French from the caravansary and taken Rosetta. Fort St Julian was bombarded by our gunboats; we heard the cannonading across the bay at Aboukir on the 17th and 18th. This fort surrendered on the 19th; it stands on the left bank of the Nile and commands the main branch of the river.

Our regiment was ordered to get ready for the march

and every one that was able to march was ordered to join. I went round to the hospital sheds and took leave of some of my wounded comrades; the plague was stealing in amongst them, and few that had limbs taken off recovered. This day I shook hands with many a one I never saw again. About this time our surgeon William Findlay who had been promoted to be Physician of the Forces, died.

CHAPTER 7

A Hot March

On the 23rd of April we marched and crossed the lake Maadie near the blockhouse which with some guns defends the entrance; there is a stockade and battery on the other side. We crossed on a large raft drawn from one side to the other with ropes fixed on supports of wood and pulled hand over hand by about twenty sturdy Arabs nearly naked and making a great noise in their own language. When we got over we travelled on a causeway composed of large blocks of stone built as a dyke to keep the sea back and answer the purposes of a road. We soon left this hard road and marched through the sand, sinking every step to the calf of the leg, until we came to the entrance of lake Elko. By this time it was dark. We got into flat bottomed boats belonging to the fleet and landed on the other side, at the caravansary, a kind of Turkish inn for travellers which the French had converted into a fort for the protection of this passage. We stuck our bayonets into the ground and slept sound after the fatiguing hot day's march. 24th to Etko a fine village but very dirty; here we made ourselves booths of the date trees, as their long branches made a good shelter from the sun and dew. The inhabitants came among us in a friendly manner selling bread, fried fish, eggs, fruit, etc. We found good water here and the Arabs came round with it in skins selling it to us. Lord Hutchinson left for El Hamet.

This being the first town I was in in this country I was curious in examining it. It stands very high, and has had a line wall round it which is now tumbling into decay. The lake is close by the south and east of it; the bay about four or five miles to the north; and nothing is to be seen growing but date trees, the only thriving article I have seen in this country. With others I visited a school and looked attentively at some boys receiving instruction from one of the lower *mufti* or clergy, a fine fatherly looking man. He showed us the books they were using, but we could make nothing of them, we supposed they might be some parts of the Koran. In writing, this was unaccountable to us, they began the line to the right and wrote towards the left to the end of the line, then began at the right again and so on; they used small reed or cane pens. The teacher was at great pains to explain things to us, and in return for his civility I showed him as I best could how we wrote and our method of teaching from a book I had in my pocket. He seemed to understand me and we parted good friends.

We then visited the mosque or place of worship. It contained no furniture except some stone benches round the walls. The pulpit which was not unlike those used at home, stood in the centre; on it lay a large book which we took to be the Alcoran. In the passage were some large stone baths filled with water, as we thought for the Turks washing before going into prayers. This place of worship was small with a lofty spire or minaret shaped on the top like a turban, but with no clock or bell, indeed I saw none of these in the country. These minarets have balustrades round them in which men are posted night and day; their duty is to call the people to prayers, proclaim the hours, and give notice of any accident that may occur. We next visited a weaver's shop; the weaver was weaving linen but not the fine linen of Egypt, for it was coarse enough. We then left this dirty village and its swarms of flies which had been buzzing about us all the time we were in it. We noticed that many of the people had sore eyes.

On Monday, 25th, we marched by the side of the lake on which some of our armed boats were sailing. Many Arabs came with pitchers of water selling a drink for a *para*. Some stout fellows among them would carry eight or ten men's knapsacks a whole day's march for ten or twelve *paras*. We now began to get clear of the sand and glad we were to get our feet on cultivated ground once more.

We got among fields of grass and corn and encamped at El Hamet where we joined the brigade under Sir John Doyle, which consisted of the 1st Royals, 30th, 90th, and 92nd regiments. General Doyle was a true, hearty Irishman, and well fitted to have command of men. He had none of that pride and sullenness which too often attend those in authority.

He was ever attentive to our wants and his affability and kindness can never be forgotten by any soldier in the brigade. And it was the same wherever he had the command. The men that mounted his guard seldom went without a glass of rum in the morning from his own hand. General Craddock's brigade consisted of 2nd or Queen's, 8th, 18th Royal Irish, and 58th regiments. The four flank companies of the 40th and the Corsican Rangers were under Colonel Spencer. The cavalry were the nth, 12th, and 26th regiments, General Finch. There were three brigades of artillery. The cavalry got all mounted on good horses and some of our artillery was drawn by bullocks, and other pieces were carried on camel's backs and covered with tarpaulin to prevent the heat of the sun from rendering the wheels and carriages unfit for service.

A bridge of boats was formed across the Nile and the 89th regiment, Colonel Lord Blaney with other troops chiefly Turks, crossed over to advance on the Delta side of the river. The Grand Bashaw arrived with the Turkish armed flotilla; he acted as Admiral and General and had his flag hoisted on one of the largest of his vessels. Captain Stephenson, R.N., had command of the British armed boats and was a more useful man for the service than the Great Turk.

This camp was about a mile and a half from Rosetta which is the chief trading town on this branch of the Nile. It has some good brick houses whitewashed over with latticed windows without glass, streets narrow and dusty and swarming with flies. The Greeks had followed us in their boats and were the chief retailers here also. A great trade seemed to be carried on in grain, and many germs or country boats are here loaded with it. The entrance into the mouth of the river below the town is difficult on account of the *Boghaz* or bar and the sand shifting from one side of the river to the other, and in a strong westerly wind it is nearly choked up; some of our armed launches had to wait some days before they could pass. The river at this place is about 200 yards broad with a steep bank and a blue -clay bottom, runs smooth, and is very muddy, yet it is the only good water in the country, is very wholesome, and is even said to be nourishing for the body. I have known some of our men drink from ten to twelve quarts of it in the course of a day's march, just as it was lifted out of the river and never heard that it hurt any one.

The heat was very oppressive and I have seen us while on the march during a halt, wringing our clothes and buff belts, they being as wet with sweat as if they had been soaked in water; they soon dried in the sun and we were never a whit the worse. This part of the country is intersected with deep canals with high banks; they were all dry at this season of the year, but when the Nile rises to its height the water flows in; the mouths of the canals are closed up and the water retained and this serves for watering the fields. No tillage is required for the first crop; when the river retires within its banks the seed is thrown among the mud and slime left behind and little else is done to produce a plentiful crop. When a second or third crop is required the land is tilled with the plough, drawn by oxen. Wheat is the chief grain raised, but I have seen plenty of barley and all other grain except oats; and at this season, standing on one of the raised banks and looking east over the river across the Delta which is level as far as the eye can reach, to see the fields bringing forth their yellow treasure is a very pleasant sight it being nigh harvest; this made us repeat the saying 'There is corn in Egypt.' We enjoyed the sight all the more from having seen little but sea and sand for a long time back.

The villages on the banks of the Nile are numerous and well inhabited; they are generally built on mounds of earth and are surrounded with a high bank to prevent the river, as we thought, from sweeping them away in the flood when it overflows. Most of the towns have a wall of bricks or mud built round to protect the inhabitants from the Bedouin Arabs, who sometimes make a rush from the desert and carry off the people and property of the village. There are no houses outside of these walls for want of security, yet their grain lies outside in heaps in the open air beside their threshing floors, where it is trodden out by oxen and other animals, and winnowed much the same as I have seen in Scotland. The heaps are divided from each other by a row of bricks or a piece of wood; they lie till a merchant is found, when the grain is carried in baskets to the boats on the river. I have taken great pleasure in sitting by the river side and seeing these mountains of corn disappearing; most of the people of the villages seemed to be employed in their embarkation; they looked poor but happy. There are many hungry looking dogs about these small towns which are turned out at night, when they make a great noise barking and howling. The Turks here do little but sit and smoke and drink coffee. The Copts, the ancient Egyptians, and the Arabs do all the servile work. The Mamelukes are gentlemen soldiers commanded by their own officers who rule the country as tyrants under the Turkish Governor who resides at Cairo.

Chapter 8

The Enemy Retire

On the 5th of May the army marched by the side of the Nile: the bank was covered with reeds and thick bushes. As there was no regular road we marched in companies or half-companies in a straight line through fine cornfields, treading down the ripe grain. Passed some large town and villages. On our approach men, women, and children got on the top of their flat-roofed houses and shouted for joy. The Turkish Bashaw's vessel was received with marks of great joy, beating of kettledrums, clashing of cymbals, and playing pipe organs, while a multitude followed on the river bank crying at the top of their voice *'O! Allah Humbo, O! Allah Humbo.'*

We saw some of the enemy's picquets who retired quietly on our advance. We encamped this day in two lines with the armed flotilla in the rear of our left. Our tents were brought from the baggage boats and pitched at night and put on board before we marched in the morning.

6th, this day the Turks took up a position in our rear next to the river; they have a great number of camels, horses and asses all in disorder. 7th, to Deirout, where some of the French had been in huts; they retreated after having set fire to the huts, which were composed of the materials of a village they had wrecked. Here we got provisions served out, and some buffaloes were killed for the use of the regiment. The flesh of this animal is coarse and soon gets black if exposed to the sun, but it eats well with a piece of salt pork, and makes excellent soup.

On the 9th we resumed our march to Rhamanieh and heard some popping of musketry on the right of our front, by the French outposts and our advanced guard. The artillery and cavalry moved to the front with Colonel Spencer's brigade and drove in the enemy's outposts to the bank of the great canal which runs through the country from the river to Alexandria, the same canal that we cut in front of our lines in order to fill the lake Mareotis. This was a fine place of defence for the enemy, as they could move their columns and artillery from right to left unobserved by us as there was no rising ground in the neighbourhood. We closed to quarter distance, threw off our knapsacks and left them with a guard, formed line among some large fields of wheat while firing was going on briskly to our right. Captain King had a leg carried off by a cannon shot, and Sergeant Clark of our light company was wounded in the jaw. The Turks formed in three lines on the left of our regiment and brought up some clumsy pieces of artillery. On them in particular the French directed their fire from Fort Rhamanieh, throwing shot and shell, which set the fields of ripe wheat on fire, this being very dry burnt with fury; the fire ran like lightning among us so we were obliged to shift our position. Our dragoons dismounted and cut lanes with their swords between the burning and the standing corn; when the flame reached these openings it generally went out.

We halted until most of the fires were extinguished and then advanced: the enemy retired behind the canal bank, raising their heads above the level and giving us a few shots as they were closing in their force to the right. Meanwhile the Turks were advancing briskly on our left, their officers or standard-bearers running to the front with the flags and holding them up, their front line formed upon them and discharged their muskets, then the flags started to the front again, and so on. This did very well till some of them got within a few yards of the canal bank, when a tremendous fire opened upon them from the fort and the French artillery and the infantry rising from behind the canal bank poured a volley among the Turks, and with a shout rushed upon them at the charge. The Turks ran like a drove of sheep, and I could see that those who carried the standards were amongst their best runners. They fell back on their 2nd and 3rd lines when they all got into confusion. The French ran after them hallooing and firing until they were checked by the fire of the gunboats on the river, and General Doyle formed an oblique line with the 30th and our regiment which fired on them as we got into the alignment facing the river. On this they ran as fast from us as they had done after the Turks. Our good and faithful allies began to entrench themselves by the river side and came back and picked up some of their wounded men; they made a great lamentation over some great personage whom they carried on board one of their vessels.

At night we lay down in our positions in the ranks, and a chain of sentinels was posted a few yards to the front. When placing them I was challenged and fired upon by some of the French vedettes. I returned no answer but drew back nearer the regiment. After it was dark the troops on the other side of the river contested a rising ground which commanded the turn of the river above the fort. After taking this all was still till about one o'clock in the morning when a gun was fired from the fort and there was a running fire from the sentinels opposite us. We jumped up in the ranks, thinking we were to be attacked, and stood to our arms but heard nothing more. When daylight appeared we saw the white flag flying on the fort and an officer with a drummer beating a parley came to our lines. They were conducted to General Hutchinson. The officer offered to surrender the fort, which contained 300 men, most of them wounded; he said their army in the field had marched off on the road for Cairo.

On the officer mentioning that the French army had escaped and that there were only 300 men in the fort, General Hutchinson got into a violent passion and it is said was only prevented by General Craddock from knocking the officer down. We halted on the 10th and the French were put on board some country germs and escorted to Aboukir by some of our armed boats. The Turks got possession of the fort and some of their numerous standards were placed on the walls. They kept firing off their muskets all day as was their practice on entering towns or villages.

The result of this day's work I never heard; but I saw two of the Turkish gunboats sunk in the river, and many Turks were killed and wounded by the river side. Our own wounded were put into boats and taken down to the General Hospital formed at Rosetta. The Grand Bashaw came on shore and pitched his tent, which for grandeur surpassed anything of the kind I ever saw. The marque was covered with red velvet lined with blue, gold tassels and fringes. The Bashaw sat in state on velvet cushions distributing rewards in money to every Turk who brought a Frenchman's head, and they were scattered through the fields in search of heads and were not very nice as to how or where they obtained them; it was said that some of our soldiers' heads were among them. I went to view the horrid spectacle of a pile of heads, and beheld with detestation the exulting manner in which they brought them in and the way they kicked them about heads of the very men who were a terror to them yesterday. He also gave money to some British women who were washing at the river.

Fort Rhamaniah is well calculated to defend the river and the entrance to the canal to Alexandria. There has been a fenced city here; the walls are built of brick with a ditch and drawbridge. There are some large brick buildings called by us granaries. Some of our people would have it that they were built by the Israelites and they look very old indeed. The French had collected a great number of boats in a creek of the river; when they retreated of course the boats fell to be divided among us. Our regiment got five of these to carry the tents and the men's knapsacks; this enabled us to march lighter and make longer stages. Reached a town called Nickle. Being a namesake of my own I paid more attention to it than I did to most of the towns. Indeed I seldom went into them for they are nearly all alike, dirty and full of vermin, with brick and mud walls; and many a farmer at home would not keep pigs in the sties in which I have seen families huddled together in the villages on the fertile banks of the Nile. Some of them no doubt contained better houses than others, with more mosques and minarets and palm trees anything beyond these had no enticement for us.

The Arabs were continually going amongst us selling bread, as much as a man could eat for two *paras*, three boiled eggs sold for the same money; water, butter or oil, and honey were carried about in skins for sale; onions, cucumbers, etc., all very cheap. Yet notwithstanding this and that our men had plenty of money some of the baser sort could not refrain from taking the goods for nothing and even beating and abusing the Arabs. When so used they made a great outcry beating their breasts and tearing their beards, and throwing dust on their heads calling out '*O! Al-lah Allah, Sultan Sultan a how* '. I have often had pity on the poor creatures when I could not assist them.

11th Shibnaghie, twelve miles from Rhamaniah. 14th Benoufar. We halted a day here to get our knapsacks ashore and wash our linen; this was quickly done as one shirt was dry before the other was washed, the heat of the sun was so great. This day I swam across the river to the Delta and bought two melons. I was much fatigued in coming back and was carried far down the stream, yet kept a firm hold of my goods. Melons became very cheap a few days after, selling for five or six *paras*: when ripe they are delightful and refreshing to a thirsty person.

CHAPTER 9

In the Desert

We encamped on the 16th at Algam where the cultivated land is narrow, and the sandy desert is gradually making it less, for the sand is continually gaining towards the
river. On the morning of the next day the 17th, as we were
going to the boats for our rations an Arab was seen riding
into the camp at full gallop with his turban flying at the end
of his lance. He was directed to the commander-in-chief's
tent, where he gave intelligence that the French were in
the desert to our right and rear. On this alarm the dragoons
and light artillery and our brigade got under arms. General
Doyle rode along the ranks and told us he would get us
bread and rum before we started, and he rode oft at full
gallop to the commissary's for that purpose but, just as he
and the rations came in sight the order to march was given,
and we entered the desert very ill prepared indeed. We followed our guide as quickly as we could and at length, after
marching seven miles, we came in sight of the enemy, who
fired upon our advanced guard and retreated but after a
few shots being fired from our artillery they surrendered.
We found them to be a party of 600 men with 550 camels,
on their way from Alexandria to Cairo for provisions. They
had a large sum of money with them but before they sur-

rendered their commissary caused it to be divided among his own men. This was the worst day's march we had in the country. Very few men had had time to get water in their canteens, at every step we sank over the ankle in light sand, and for three paces to the front we slid one back. The sun was very hot and not a breath of wind. Hundreds of our people dropped down and had to be taken up by the camels and I am sorry to say that some of the men of our brigade while in this helpless condition were killed by the Bedouin Arabs for the sake of their arms and accoutrements. On our return we met some Turks coming to our assistance with many camels and horses bearing skins of water. This was a blessed relief; we all drank greedily; our throats being so parched it was long before we were satisfied, and in the hurry much of the precious water was spilt. No tree nor bush nor any herbage grows here; sand, nothing but sand and sunshine. Sometimes you think you see water before you at a distance. 'A lake, a lake!' cry some of our people, in a short time it is gone, but it appears again and again; it is a strange illusion.

We got out of the sand about 6 o'clock in the evening. On the plain we fell in with some sort of fig trees, the fruit having a notch on one side; we devoured every one we could reach. We escorted our prisoners to the river where they were embarked in boats, then returned to our tents and found that the men who went for the rations had done their duty; every camp kettle was full of water and our rum and provisions ready. When the roll was called of our company one half was absent: they all joined during the night.

A camel park was formed under charge of Captain John MacLean of our regiment and Sergeants James Clark and Alexander MacLean went as assistants to him. Each regiment got camels to carry the tents in lieu of the boats which were sent down the river with the prisoners. Our officers got some good horses and asses, and the soldiers' wives were provided with these latter animals which are very large and superior to any we had ever seen. But they caused a great noise in the camp in the night time, for when one began to bray they all got on the same tune and disturbed our sleep much. At Algam were the greatest flocks of pigeons I ever saw or ever will see I believe. The town is surrounded with dovecotes built round from top to bottom with earthen pots; in these pots they breed and hatch their young. The Turks kept firing at them most of the time we were here no sparing of ammunition with the Turk. We had to wait three days here for bread and when we got it we found it coarse rusks, as hard as bricks which had to be steeped in water before we could use them.

We had one day's hot wind from the south (23rd May) which will ever be remarkable to the Egyptian army. The morning was lowering and the sun was of a blood red colour. It began to blow about 9 o'clock: and woe be to him that is far from shelter, as neither man nor beast can survive in it three days! It came from the desert as hot as the opening of an oven door, bringing small sand like mist along with it. All our sentinels were called in and the cattle crept close to the ground and groaned for fear. The buffaloes took to the river, covering themselves all but the nose in the water; flesh putrefied; any metal substance could not be touched with the naked hand; and no man was able to stir out of his tent until the evening when happily the wind changed to the north- west.

We crossed a neck of sand and passed a deserted village which had been overflowed with this shifting sand. On this march we heard that a Turkish army had marched from Syria into Egypt by way of Salehieh and Belbeis. We encamped on the 28th at Manouff, a large town where the French had a garrison. It stands on the left bank of the river, near where it divides, one branch flowing to Damietta, the other to Rosetta, and enclosing what is called the Delta, the most fertile part of the country. A canal here unites the two branches. This day we took a prize of five boats laden with stores, shoes, and money; they had got on the wrong branch of the river, and missed the French who were retiring before us. General Menou's lady was in one of these boats; she was a native of this country and lately married to the French commander-in-chief: she was sent to him at Alexandria. We were not permitted to take any article from the boats, though shoes were in great demand among us; but when our faithful allies the Turks arrived they took whatever they wanted.

THE PLAGUES OF EGYPT

This part of the country so abounded with frogs that it was impossible to get at the water in the river without treading upon them, and from their slimy nature many a tumble some of our men got: after dark they croaked so as to be heard at a considerable distance from the river. So some of the plagues of Moses exist here yet. The flies are in swarms about the towns; you must keep your hands in motion to prevent them going down your throat or into your eyes. In some places the ground was black with fleas, especially in places where the French had been in camp. As for sand lice, when the date trees were split at Aboukir for making the general hospital, I have seen so many in the hearts of them that they might have been gathered in handfuls.

One day locusts passed from west to east in such numbers as to darken the air; while as to boils, few of the army that marched to Cairo escaped them. I myself suffered from this trouble and also from prickly heat but was forced to do my duty with them the best way I could, and some days that was bad enough.

Marched forward to Mishlee and encamped. On 1st June we were joined here by Mamelukes under command of Ibrahim Bey, fine looking soldiers indeed. Many of them were mounted on those running camels or dromedaries, with all the luxury the country can afford, dressed in fine silk robes, fitter for a court than a camp, with red velvet saddles and silver rings in the noses of their camels and with silk cords to guide them. At a distance they looked like a lot of women; yet they are said to be brave in the field. Each of them has an Arab or two running in the rear on foot carrying lances which they throw with great dexterity from their camels or dromedaries, and are sure of their object at 30 or 40 yards distance; I have often seen them at practice at their camp at Cairo.

Our army marched past in open columns of companies with drums beating and I am certain they could think no less of us than we of them as they sat on their camels smoking. This day while marching in companies some men on the right of our company fell in to a slime pit; the sun dried the clay upon their clothes and they were droll figures.

4th June to Lochmas; 5th, Ouardan; 7th, Gatta; 8th Burlos; 14th Saael; 16th to a place almost within reach of the enemy's guns. Here we were joined by the 28th and 42nd regiments, which had marched from Alexandria in twelve days. 18th, came in sight of the Pyramids, the two large ones: this cheered us on.

On the 21st we halted within two miles of Gizeh and encamped with the enemy to our front; threw a bridge of boats across the Nile and raised batteries on each side for its protection. A line of dried buffalo skins was stretched on stakes, musket proof at 30 yards distance. All stores and baggage were halted below the bridge.

The Grand Vizier's army arrived on the other side of the Nile, nearly opposite to us, and a great multitude they appeared to be. With tents and marquees pitched without order, camels, horses, asses, Arabs, they covered a great extent of ground. There was little subordination or regularity among them. Some of our artillerymen who had been at Constantinople instructing the Turks appeared here like gentlemen. I went over to the Turkish camp with Corporals Sinclair and Innes of our company, drank some very strong coffee, and got two whiffs of an opium pipe, which some of the Turks smoke until they are intoxicated. As the bridge of boats was a ready means of communication between the two camps many of the Turks came over to look at the people who could beat the French.

The whole army advanced and drove in the French outposts. They disputed the ground on the east bank of the river with the Turks and kept up a heavy cannonade upon them from a battery at a windmill; this kept them at bay. We marched on and took up our position with our left opposite the centre of Gizeh and at a great distance from the river, for the French had fortified the banks as well as Rodda Island in the middle of the river. Some heavy guns were brought up from our flotilla. We were joined by the 42nd, 79th, and 90th regiments under command of General Oakes. It was reported that the Indian army under General Baird had sailed up the Red Sea and landed at Cosseir and Suez, marched across the desert, and was driving the French down the river.

Thus being fairly hemmed in on all sides the enemy offered on the 22nd to capitulate to the British generals only. This was agreed to, and a large marquee was pitched between Gizeh or what was called the Horse Barracks, and our front line. The staff of both armies met accompanied by a guard of twelve men from each, who were very friendly with one another. The capitulation being signed and hostages exchanged the French were to march to the seaside and embark with their arms and ammunition, bag and baggage, and to be taken to the nearest port in France in our ships at the expense of the British Government. I believe they were very glad to return to their country. This was done 27th June 1801. On the 29th General Moore joined us, having now recovered from his wound received on 21st March.

CHAPTER 10

On the Banks of Nile

On the 6th of July the British troops were reviewed by the Grand Vizier, a fresh looking middle-aged man, with a great retinue of Bashaws, Agas, etc. He was escorted by a squadron of the 12th Light Dragoons. We received him with presented arms. He rode along the line and looked very attentively at us. We then marched past with drums beating and music playing. From his gestures he seemed to be well pleased notwithstanding our ragged condition. Our chief guide and interpreter dressed in scarlet and with a regulation feather in his cap rode between Lord Hutchinson and the Grand Vizier. We received the thanks of the Commander-in-chief for turning out in such good order and having so cleanly an appearance before the Turkish commander. This day the French removed the remains of General Kleber their late Commander-in-chief who had been assassinated by a fanatic Turk; minute guns were fired by them as he was borne along.

The thanks of both Houses of Parliament were read to us on 8th July for our meritorious conduct in landing in Egypt and for our conduct on the 13th and 21st of March. A general promotion took place among the officers; General Hutchinson was raised to the peerage and many of the Generals were made Knights of the Bath, etc.

With some others I obtained a pass to view the Pyramids. We started at reveille in the morning, and reached a small village called Haurige where we hired an Arab for five *paras* each, there might be about twenty of us, to guide us over and into the Pyramid. We soon reached this stupendous second wonder of the world, but as every Gazetteer gives an account of these Pyramids I need say little. They stand about 9 miles from the bed of the river and about 5 from the right of our camp, but the ground being so level it appears to the eye to be not more than 2 miles. We resolved to have an outside view first. The Great Pyramid is built of very large stones from 12 to 1 8 feet long and 4 feet and upwards thick; these form irregular steps to the summit, which is level and may be about 36 feet square. A great many names are here cut out by different visitors; I wrought very hard and got D. NICOL, 92 REGT carved, and broke my knife while finishing the job; this is on the southeast corner, and is likely to stand some time.

The greater part of the French army marched and encamped along the great plain, with their left to the Pyramids, and the 79th's grenadier company did duty on the bridge of boats built by the French between Gizeh and Cairo. The Turks entered the city, hallooing and firing their muskets, and making all the noise a disorderly mob was fit to do. Sir David Baird's army occupied Rodda Island and some barracks opposite our left on the other side of the river. It consisted of some troops of the 8th Light Dragoons, 10th, 19th, 61st and 88th regiments, with some of the East India Company Artillery and a few battalions of Sepoys, the first I ever saw. They were fine stout-looking men, and when off duty wore nothing but a very short pair of drawers, which gave them an odd appearance to us.

July 11th, I mounted Sir John Doyle's guard with six men. We had to strike his marquee and pack his baggage on two camels to go into Cairo as he had that morning obtained leave to return to Europe on account of sickness. I crossed the bridge of boats built by the French and entered into a mass of confusion, the French with their baggage marching out and the Turks marching in.

The streets in Cairo are narrow and we were like to be choked with the dust or squeezed against the brick houses. At length the street got quite blocked up; there were so many animals, camels, mules, and asses, that no movement could be made one way or other, but a party of Turkish cavalry going my way cleared a passage by blows on every poor Arab who had charge of a beast, whether in fault or not. I got our camels into the wake of the cavalry and in a little time after saw Sir John's aide-de-camp, his nephew, looking out for us. He kept by us until we reached an open square with some large brick buildings; into one of these we entered and found ourselves in a fine courtyard planted with trees and a fountain in the centre. I asked permission to visit the castle, as we were not far from it. This the aide-de-camp granted but said we must be in our camp by sunset. Off we set for the castle or citadel which is very large, standing on a height in a fine commanding situation, but I think it could be commanded by the hill to the south of it.

At the west side stand some fine buildings with trees, the principal magazines and stores. The French had a mint and a printing office here. Saw many piles of shells made of a bluish kind of marble which must have been hollowed out with great labour, and many large mortars for discharging them. Also piles of new made shot of brass and copper. I should not wonder if the Turks have them carried off for gold, as they have done the brass works of a gun which the French constructed, and which fired every day at 12 o'clock by the heat of the sun through a burning glass just over the touch hole.

Most of the shops were shut, the merchants preferring to take their goods to the British bazaar rather than trust the Turks who at almost every open door were to be seen drinking sherbet and smoking. We were right glad when we got out of the confusion and gained the end of the bridge where we turned our backs on Grand Cairo, with its narrow streets, brick and mud buildings, and its poor half-naked inhabitants.

15th July, all the arrangements for the march down the country were now completed. The French that surrendered and marched out of Cairo on 9th July amounted to about 13,000 under command of General Belliard. Some Greeks and Copts in their service got liberty to go to France if they chose. The British took up their position in front, the French were placed in the centre and the Indian army in the rear. The boats belonging to each division kept the same order on the river. The Mamelukes kept on the left and the Turkish Albanian regiments marched regularly on the other side of the river. A party of French dragoons with some of ours and our quartermaster general took up the alignment of the camp.

At daybreak on the 15th a gun was fired and we all got on the move. A strict eye was kept on the French, for we were not sure of them although the treaty was signed. No accident occurred. When we came within seven miles of Rosetta on the 28th we took up a strong position on the plain with a high canal bank on our right and left. Our cannon were pointed and matches burning and strong guards sent to the front. The French then marched past, between us and the river, in open order of companies with about sixty pieces of cannon, all the cannoniers fine looking men well clothed, mounted on asses. Their 14th and 22nd regiments of dragoons were allowed to be the finest cavalry we had ever seen, and I have no doubt they showed themselves to the best advantage while passing the British army. They all marched on to the sea-side to embark. It was feared by some of our people that they would start off across the country to Alexandria, but I never believed they had any such intention, as they seemed very glad to get home to their own country.

On the 29th, General Hutchinson, who had been left behind at Cairo, arrived. We encamped about 2 miles above Rosetta where the ground was covered with black beetles, which annoyed us very much. The Nile had swollen greatly since we commenced our march down the country. Most of the canals began to fill and those drawn between the river and the lake began to run like mill-courses, and the water was very thick and muddy for drinking. The river so gained on us that we were forced to remove our camp to the edge of the sandhills below Rosetta among some date trees, where we were in no danger of being carried away by the flood.

On the 31st the French began to embark and the embarkation continued for ten days. A great number of women, natives of the country accompanied the French to the seaside, but they were not allowed to embark except a very few who could show that they were lawfully married; the rest were left to find their way home as they best could.

General Lawson, R.A., took two guns from the French which had been taken from our army in the retreat from Dunkirk; he claimed them as British property. Our cavalry were all fresh mounted by the horses of the French dragoons, which were far superior to any we had. Our artillery horses were replaced, and Donald Macintosh of our company went as an artillery driver, one man was sent from each company. At this time Sergeant Symon of our company died, also Strongale Rab and Robert Cameron, Earl of Alkmaar, all great personages in the regiment. The Arabs who had attended the French army began to flock about our camp and also some of their women who had been turned back on their embarking.

As we passed along the inhabitants of the villages seemed to rejoice that the war in their country was at an end. They would call out *'Tieb tieb Anglo, Francois, Turk, soa, soa.'* This as far as we could understand means, 'Good good English, French and Turks the same and the same.' But if you asked them for a drink of water they would hold out their hand and say *'Had fluce a para,'* and if you said *'Ma fish fluce,'* they would say *'Ma fish moy,'* and point to the river, if you said 'No money,' they said 'No water,' or 'You may go to the river.'

Our brigade was inspected by Lord Hutchinson who ordered us camels to carry our packs to Alexandria but Colonel Spencer said there was no need for it. This officer had had command of the brigade since General Doyle left and what different treatment we received, the one always looking out for the comfort of the soldiers, the other harassing us as far as he thought we would bear it. Marched, and the lake being much overflowed by the rising of the Nile we were obliged to march among the sand, whereas if we had started early in the morning this might have been avoided. Many of our men fell behind, for water was scarce. We encamped at Etko and surrounded the wells. I sat by one of them and drank water more than I had done since I came to the country. I thought I was never to be satisfied, and my eyes were getting dim for want of it. On August we came upon the great causeway leading from Rosetta; it is about 1 2 feet broad: thought it must have been the main road to Alexandria. Came to the seaside once more and thought ourselves refreshed by the air from it. Crossed at the caravansary on a bridge of boats, halted an hour and had a scramble for some brackish water. Reached the block-house where we offered some Turks money for water, half a dollar for a canteenful. A rush was made upon the Turks, they were knocked over and their water taken from them. This day some men of our brigade dropped down dead while marching in the ranks. I happened to have good luck: being on the right of the company my feet were kept moist all day with the salt water. We met the 22nd Light Dragoons just landed from Britain; they were mounted on French horses, having arrived just in time to receive them. We crossed on the raft at the mouth of the lake and halted by the wells we dug before the battle of the 13th March. Next day, August 9th, we marched into the lines and took up our station on the left of the Grand Fort. Great alterations had been made since we were here; deep trenches were cut, breastworks raised, pits dug in front to prevent an attack from cavalry, redoubts well finished and mounted with heavy cannon from the fleet from the sea to the lake. Wells had been built by new troops from Britain, 20th, 24th, 26th, 27th, and the Loyal Irish Fencibles. Detachments had arrived for all the regiments; we got sixty men for ours. Everything appeared in a state of security; officers' marquees were screened by date branches and gravel walks made round them very comfortable indeed. Here was an excellent market formed on the left of the line, in which all the produce of the country was exposed for sale; it was under the superintendence of Sergeant-major Miles of the 28th regiment who was made provost-marshal. A wine store was erected and on a pass signed by an officer four canteens were filled for a Spanish dollar. Bridges were made across the cuts made in the canal for joining the two lakes.

CHAPTER 11

The Siege of Alexandria

On the 16th of August in the evening, the armed launches and flat-bottomed boats were assembled to the left of the line. The greater part of the troops last arrived from Britain and the Guards, with some artillery, embarked under command of Sir Eyre Coote, and sailed after dark up the lake Mareotis, and got quietly landed to the west of Alexandria about daybreak, while we made a diversion in their favour in front. About two hours before daybreak we marched into the plain in three divisions, one by the sea-side, one in the centre of the plain, and one on the left by the lake side under General Doyle who had again joined us. After passing our advanced posts in silence the enemy fired into us. We formed in line in rear of what we called the Green Hill and brought up our artillery and stood under arms till daylight when the French marched in columns in front of their batteries to oppose our division in the centre of the plain. The 30th regiment advanced to check a party of the enemy advancing from the bridge towards the hill when a smart firing commenced. General Doyle desired us to lie close to the ground until ordered to rise, telling us in an Irish whisper to level low, for said he, one bullet in a Frenchman's shin bone this day is as good as two in his head some other time. The enemy drove in the 30th regiment. We were ordered to advance and when we began to move received the fire of all their guns that could bear upon us, as well as a volley of small arms from the division coming towards us. This we returned in good earnest. On this the enemy retreated under shelter of their guns and we were ordered back to screen ourselves as much as possible from the fire of their heavy cannon, which kept playing most of the day. A shot knocked away Colonel Napier's horse's hind leg, and threw the Colonel on his back among the sand. The Colonel sat up on the sand, and called out to get the saddle and bridle and he would get another horse. A cannon shot struck a white stone in front of me, which flew in pieces and hurt some of the right of our company about the neck and face, while a tooth was knocked right down my throat with a bit of it. I had good reason to thank God things were no worse with me.

The division on the right kept disputing a round hill nearly opposite us most of the day; it remained in our possession at night. The centre division having no shelter on the plain was drawn back to our lines. We lost between thirty and forty men of our brigade in this affair; working parties with entrenching tools were ordered out to us in the afternoon, to throw up breastworks and entrenchments along the brow of the hill. The enemy kept up a constant fire upon them until they reached us, doing them much damage. This party consisted of the Irish Fencible regiment and they never having seen anything of the kind before, were rather amazed poor lads. About this time some Arabs ventured out amongst us to sell bread, which they carried in baskets. It was soon bought and they sat down on a bank of sand exposed to the French lines to count their gains, when a 24lb shot struck the bank and almost buried the Arabs in the sand. None of them were seriously hurt. After shaking themselves they ran off leaving baskets, turbans, and money behind, crying out 'O *Allah, Francois*,' etc.; our division never got such a hearty laugh together since we came to the country. No more Arabs appeared this day.

After dark we were relieved by the centre division. On the 18th, our regiment struck their tents and moved into the plain in rear of the Green Hill. At this place the ground was covered with fine salt about 6 inches deep incrusted by the sun. On the 19th, all our troops were drawn across the plain. We thought we were to storm the town, and I am certain the French thought the same. As we advanced their sentinels fired and retreated. We fired none, as we were ordered not to fire on any account. The alarm being given, the enemy opened a tremendous fire of shot and shell; from the seaside to the lake seemed in a blaze, and the air was full of shells; they dropped them so as to clear their own works, for they certainly thought we were upon them. But not a shot was returned by us, except by some of our skirmishers in front who were close on their works. This was a false attack on our part, made to enable Sir Eyre Coote's troops to take possession of a height which commands the western harbour of Alexandria. This they did and threw up a blue light as a signal; on this we marched back to our tents about daybreak.

We did duty by brigades at the advanced posts. A road was made on the left by the side of the lake, and heavy cannon were mounted on two batteries erected on the hill, and on two by the seaside. It was a fatiguing job getting the heavy guns to the batteries through the deep sand, and this had to be done in the night time. We got everything ready to commence firing on the 1st of September, which we did powerfully from every gun that could be brought to bear. Our war vessels stood as close in to the harbour as they could; some very heavy metal was opened on them from Pharaoh's Castle. Our gunboats on the lake kept up a constant fire on the right of the enemy's lines, while General Coote's batteries joined in from the western side of the town. All this made the place hot enough for them. One of our twenty-four pounders on the left battery burst and killed and wounded some of the artillery.

On the 27th, in the evening an officer came from General Menou with a letter asking a cessation of hostilities for three days that he might draw up articles of capitulation. This was agreed to. On the 29th an extension of time for thirty-six hours was asked. General Hutchinson sent back word that if the articles of capitulation were not sent in by twelve o'clock that night, our batteries would open and the place be stormed. About 10 o'clock a message was sent by the French General that the articles would be ready the next day. After some delay the articles were signed by Lord Hutchinson, and on 2nd September by Lord Keith who came ashore for that purpose. It was stipulated that our army should take possession of the outworks, and the French be drawn within the walls of the town till they were ready to embark. At twelve o'clock the grenadiers of our different regiments, Sir John Hope riding in front, began to cross the plain with bands playing the Grenadier March, while the troops of both armies stood looking on, they had such a noble, majestic appearance on entering the French lines. The four flags hoisted at the main entrance into the enemy's lines, the French, the Dutch, the Spanish, and one for Egypt, said to be Coptic, were struck, to be hoisted no more and the white flag displayed. In the evening the Grenadiers were relieved by the following regiments: 2nd or Queen's, 79th, and our regiment, extending from the little Pharos tower to the main entrance; a brigade of heavy artillery pointed to the Rosetta gate, on one of the guns was hoisted the British flag; on the height in rear of the wells was General Stewart's foreign brigade. The evening gun was fired before our regiment sent out their watering parties; they were turned back by Sir John Hope when within 300 yards of the wells: this kept us badly off for water during the night. We did duty here along with the French, they in the inside of the gates, and we without and we were very familiar together. The French officers and a proportion of men had liberty to go to our market and make purchases, as they had been on low diet for some time back. They came among us disposing of watches and gold rings very cheap, some of their Italian plunder I have no doubt. Some of our men taken prisoners in the month of March were sent in to our lines; they looked as if they had been badly kept, were like skeletons, dirty and ragged. While digging in the sand some of our men discovered a canvas hose charged with gunpowder leading to a 13 inch shell, from that to another, and so on extending on both sides of the main entrance into the enemy's works, on the very ground where our tents stood. As this was thought to be some piece of French treachery it was inquired into, and it was explained that it was laid there in case the British had stormed the place. The shells were dug up and collected in one place in case of any accident.

The French had very strong fortifications here. On the heights from the sea to the lake was one entire battery with a deep ditch about 18 feet broad, and *palisadoes*, and in the hollow between the walls of the town and this fortification the French lay in huts. If we had stormed these outworks we would have been exposed to the fire of the citadel and forts Cretain and Caffarelli as well as from the walls of Alexandria, which are about 30 feet high and flanked with towers, which in some places are falling into decay.

On the 11th of September the French marched out at twelve o'clock at night. We stood under arms until they passed, about 11,000 of all descriptions, on their way to embark at Aboukir. This put a finish to our labour in this country, and we had now some time to look about us for we had lain every night fully accoutred and with our fire-locks by our side since we came up here. We were ordered to take down the French huts in our rear and build two huts for each company, but with these materials were brought such a quantity of fleas that we could not get peace to sleep quietly afterwards. We now got plenty of firewood, an article we had been very scarce of in this country: villages have often been unroofed to supply fuel for the army. Flour was served out in place of bread, which was much against us as we had no way to keep it clear of sand, our method was to make dumplings of it and boil them in the camp kettles. On the 27th it was my turn to draw the company's rum. Corporal MacBean went for me, and coming back at full speed one of the cords of Mr Mackay's tent took his feet, he fell and all the liquor was sunk in the sand in a moment. He generously offered to purchase two dollars' worth of date brandy: this we all rejected.

On the 4th of October, Lieutenant Ranald MacDonald, who was our acting adjutant, ordered me to get six men and four camels to take the officers' baggage to the commissary depot, where I was to get a boat to take it on board. When I reached there I found Adjutant Campbell, and all the sick of the brigade, and learned that the regiment was to be embarked on board the *Renommee*, forty-four, and *Modeste* frigates, five companies in each. I delivered over the camels and got a boat on the 5th. We wrought very hard all morning putting the baggage into the boat, keeping each ship's baggage as much by itself as we could. We had very poor assistance. The boat was overloaded and could not get off, so we had to strip naked and push her out into the lake where deep water was: she got on several shoals and we had to again push her off until we got into the bay. I got a very severe headache and pain in the brow by over-exertion in the heat of the sun; this terminated in sore eyes. I regretted much that I was taking this disease the very last day I was in the country, for I had been exceedingly healthy since we landed in March, but I was not permitted to pass out of the house of bondage without affliction.

We reached the *Renommee* frigate after dark, and got part of the baggage on board. Early next morning we went to the *Modeste* frigate, where I delivered over my charge to Mr Donald MacBarnet, formerly quartermaster sergeant, but who has now got a commission, while poor John Macintosh, Sergeant-Major, who was wounded and present with the regiment during the campaign was entirely overlooked. On the 6th of October the five companies came on board commanded by Major Gordon. They were much fatigued with a long march through the sand, but as it was the first step on the road home they stood it with the greater fortitude.

The Gordon Highlanders
in Spain

CHAPTER 1

The Invalid Detachment

It was in 1808 that Napoleon, roused to frenzy by the news of the advance of Sir John Moore, declared that he would chase the British armies from the Peninsula. At that moment he commanded two hundred thousand veteran troops, while Moore could only gather from his scattered garrisons a fighting force of twenty-three thousand men. With these he struck vigorously at the armies commanded by Soult and Ney. In consequence Napoleon changed his plans, and when his generals reported to him that the passes were blocked with snow, he answered that if the British troops could face the rigours of the winter march in the mountains, the men under his command must do likewise, and so, with the loss of many men and animals, the passes were traversed.

Meanwhile the Spanish armies, upon whose support General Moore had relied rapidly dwindled away, and Moore having by his attack upon Bonaparte's communications succeeded for the time in saving southern Spain, recalled his advance guard and prepared to retreat. The story of what followed is too well known to need repetition here. In the trying marches and continuous fighting of the next four weeks the newly raised regiment the 92nd or Gordon Highlanders bore their part nobly, and in the battle of Corunna held the post of honour on the left wing. Their losses on that occasion were heavy and included their leader the popular Colonel Napier of Blackstone, an excellent officer.

Previous to the attack of Moore on Napoleon's communications, the British army had been quartered in all the principal towns in the south and west of Spain and of Portugal and in Lisbon large numbers of invalids and convalescents had been assembled. When the news of Napoleon's advance reached Lisbon, these parties and detachments were formed into two battalions of about eleven hundred men each; one company of the first battalion was composed solely of men from the 92nd regiment, the other companies were made up of men belonging to the 42nd, 79th, and gist Highlanders, besides some Rifles.

Colonel Greenhill-Gardyne the latest historian of the Gordons, in his most interesting and elaborate work, completed in 1903, has omitted to refer to this company, although in a footnote he mentions the fact that some of the invalids of the regiment had joined what were called the 'Corps of detachments.' The work done by the detached company has however, fortunately been preserved for us in the hitherto unpublished journal of an ex-sergeant of the regiment, who was with it during the time it formed part of the army commanded by Sir Arthur Wellesley, who had just landed at Mondego Bay.

The crisis in the history of Europe at that moment was intense, for the Germans and Austrians had risen in arms against their French conquerors; and if the British Government had only sent an adequate force into Spain to support the rising of their Spanish and Portuguese allies, there is little doubt that five years' fighting in the Peninsula would have been prevented. Instead however, of providing an adequate force, the Ministers resolved to subdivide their magnificent army of ninety thousand men. This force the Duke of York had collected so that it might be immediately available to strike at whichever point should prove to be the most vulnerable in the armour of the French Colossus, but the Government dispatched a portion of it on the hapless expedition to Walcheren and Antwerp, and sent a second corps to Sicily. Wellesley was thus compelled to accept the command of a force of only twenty thousand men, with which to secure the liberties of twelve millions of Spaniards and to overcome the combined armies of France, at that moment ten times more numerous than his own.

Nicol entered upon his experiences in the Peninsula, which are detailed with so much graphic power in his very interesting manuscript, shortly after the ignominious convention of Cintra, which for a time liberated Portugal. Incidentally it also saved the French armies at a moment when they might have fallen an easy prey as prisoners into the hands of the newly arrived and highly organised British forces.

While in Lisbon he saw the departure of the Russian fleet, consisting of seven large vessels of the line and a frigate, which had been blockaded in the river by the British fleet, under Sir Charles Cotton, and which in terms of the Convention were allowed to set sail with the Russian colours flying; all to the intense indignation of the soldiers and sailors, who regarded the fleet as a lawful prize stolen from them in the moment of victory.

From August till October 1808, the regiment lay in the neighbourhood of Lisbon; and it was on the 1st October, that while on picquet-duty in a ploughed field, Nicol was forced to remain all night exposed to the rain and wind, which produced a fever and invalided him for two months. Meantime the regiment marched into Spain and in the following month began the retreat to Corunna. From the regiment Nicol received the letter of an old comrade telling of his arrival at the Escurial near Madrid, and reporting the approach of the French, who were now advancing under Napoleon, by way of Valladolid. 'We will defeat them,' said the letter-writer, 'with the help of the Spanish army, and return to England by way of France.' This prophetic utterance, which was realised in 1814, was the last communication that Nicol had with his regiment for many years.

CHAPTER 2

The Passage of the Douro

The invalids of the 92nd left in Portugal formed a company of the first battalion of detachments, which was commanded by Lieutenant-Colonel Bunbury and Major Ross. The company of Gordons consisted of Captain Logic, Lieutenant Cattanach, Lieutenant Durie, Surgeon Beattie, eight sergeants, a piper, and seventy-six rank and file.

Sir Arthur Wellesley who landed on the 22nd April 1809, marched on the main road direct to Oporto, and came up on several occasions, with the enemy under Soult. The Portuguese troops under Marshal Beresford joined in the march, and a battalion of these under British officers, was added to each brigade of the British army.

The company of Gordons was associated with a battalion commanded by Colonel Doyle, formerly a lieutenant of the Gordons when in Egypt, and he found that nearly a dozen of the men in the company had already served with him there. Nicol tells us that the old comrades gladly drank the health of their colonel and that of his uncle Sir John Doyle, with whom they had also seen service. On 12th May 1809, at about three in the morning, an explosion was heard which made the company stand to its arms, and this proved to be caused by the blowing up of the bridge across the Douro by the French army, which had entered Oporto and sought to cover its retreat.

Wellesley determined to force the passage of the river at all costs, and having then got the enemy on the retreat to keep at them. He accordingly at once prepared to cross the great river. The Gordons marched into Villa Nova and joined General Sherbrooke's brigade which had landed in boats from Ovar.

So close was the pursuit of the French that Nicol tells us that 'if our artillery horses had been able to drag forward the guns, they would have taken many prisoners and have entered Oporto pell-mell with the French.' The enemy, however, had taken possession of all the boats they could discover, and the British fleet moved accordingly close into the mouth of the river and provided boats for the crossing. The Gordons' detachment, with two regiments, marched in double-quick time to the Sera convent, which the French had fortified and mounted with cannon, but which had been abandoned. 'We trailed arms and ran up the riverside through a firwood to a creek, where we found some large boats manned by Portuguese.' In them they crossed the river, when the French came fiercely upon them in two large columns with cannon. The enemy were driven from the top of the bank, which was held by the Gordons till the Guards and the Third Buffs had almost crossed the river, when Nicol's battalion charged the French columns and the 14th Dragoons attacked the French left and put them to rout with great slaughter. The inhabitants of Braga cheered the British troops as they approached, and took the opportunity of killing all the wounded Frenchmen they came upon, and stripping them.

After following the retreating Frenchmen for about a league, the British troops were recalled to Oporto. In the fighting the battalion had lost sixty men; and when they had got to quarters Sir Arthur addressed them and expressed how thankful he was to them for the way in which they had crossed the river, and enabled the other regiments to follow so easily.

Nicol makes this remark in passing, that 'Marshal Soult was neither prepared to defend Oporto nor to retreat out of it, but seemed as if taken by surprise or confounded at our impudence in crossing the river in the face of the whole French army.'

At night the city was illuminated, and the men-of-war boats formed a bridge of boats by which on the following day all the cannon and cavalry were transferred to the north side.

When the regiment marched from Oporto Lieutenant John Durie was left behind sick, and the following day the same fate befell 'the good Captain Logic, which every man in the company was sorry for, the more so as no officer of the 92nd was left with them, and they soon felt the want of him.'

The French army succeeded in escaping over the mountains, to the extreme annoyance of Sir Arthur and the British troops, who blamed Marshal Beresford and the Portuguese, who had been posted in the passes to prevent this. 'But for this,' Nicol says:

Soult's whole army would have been taken, as well as their guns and baggage. Negligence or mismanagement there was somewhere; but these things are not easily proved when committed by the higher powers. Beresford was challenged, and we heard no more of it; but General Toilson was sent back to England.

This, however, is only a soldier's surmise, as we know that it was the advance of Marshal Victor which compelled Sir Arthur to turn from the pursuit of Soult and join the Spanish General Cuesta, who had now reformed his force after being heavily defeated by Victor.

By the end of the month the troops had again marched . . .

. . . . over the bridge of boats across the broad and rapid Douro, and bade adieu to Oporto for ever, with its churches, convents, and port wine. To the last the British troops paid more devotion than to the first.

The Gordons had an unpleasant experience in crossing the broad, navigable lake between Ovar and Aveiro, for when they had embarked in boats which were crowded, they were very uncomfortable, and the rain came on, with a high wind, so that many of the boats were blown ashore, and the rest did not reach Aveiro till the forenoon of the following day. On landing, Sir Arthur Wellesley at their head, they were joyfully received by the inhabitants with a salute of twenty-one guns. After marching through Coimbra, they reached the river Mondego on the 4th June, when the King's Birthday was celebrated by a bathe in the river and the distribution of a pint of wine to each of the men. Now began the famous march which ended in the victory at Talavera, fought on the 27th and 28th July 1809, when the combined forces under Wellesley completely defeated the French army commanded by Joseph Bonaparte, ex-King of Naples, now King of Spain.

It was for this great victory that Sir Arthur was created a peer under the title of Lord Wellington, and it is well worthy of being recorded that the Gordons had a distinct share in the honours of the day. Nicol's description of the battle is full of interest. He tells us that the army crossed the Guadiana and entered Spain with light hearts. He begins by giving a detailed statement of the officers commanding the various divisions and brigades, and supplies particulars of all the regiments in the army, which had an effective strength of twenty thousand men.

The approach of the Spanish army is well described by Nicol, who says:

We got into a fine cultivated plain, when the French began to make their appearance in our front. Sir Arthur with his staff passed us, and we halted an hour at a village, where our cavalry dismounted and cut down some fields of ripe corn for forage. At this time we began to see great clouds of dust on the right of the plain. This was the Spanish army advancing. They had crossed the Tagus by the bridge at Almarez, and were now marching on the high-road to Madrid, driving the French outposts before them. Big words were now spoken by the boasters of taking Madrid, beating the French, and driving them out of Spain great things that were not accomplished till years after.

We halted on the 21st, and were ordered to appear as clean as possible, to be reviewed by the Spanish General Cuesta, commanding the army with which we were to act. Our army was drawn up in line. Sir Arthur and Cuesta, arrived on the ground, escorted by a troop of British and one of Spanish cavalry; they rode along the line, we paying them all military honours. Cuesta was a fine, stout, rough looking old man. He said he was happy to see us look so well after so long a march. We got one day's biscuit served out here; this was the last regular rations served out to our brigade.

On the 22nd we marched past the Spanish Grand army, as the French were in front, we were going to set them an example by commencing an attack on the enemy, for we thought that General Victor would give battle in front of Talavera. The Spaniards amounting it was said, to fifty thousand men, were drawn up on both sides of the road as we passed; they had some very heavy cannon too unwieldy for the field and many wagons, baggage-mules, asses, etc. This day was very warm, with much dust, and little or no water to be got. On the right side of the road was a stagnant pool; the cavalry rode through it, and some of our men went up to the knees amongst it drinking, though it was as thick as water-gruel.

CHAPTER 3

The Great Fight At Talavera

The French were drawn up in line about a league from Talavera. The attack was begun about eleven o'clock by the British artillery and our cavalry under General Anson, who turned the right of the French army, while the Spaniards under Duke Albuquerque, one of the best of the Spanish Generals, drove them back and through the town. Some houses and a field of wheat took fire, and the French retreated through the smoke to a position on the other side of the river Alberche, and broke down the bridge. The combined armies bivouacked in the vineyards and olive-grounds; the Spaniards in the town and by the side of the river Tagus, over which was a wooden bridge that kept communication with the country on the right bank of the river. Sir Arthur had a narrow escape this day. While reconnoitring, a cannon-shot was fired at him which carried away a branch of the tree under which he stood, within a few inches of his head a lucky escape for him. He was fully determined to bring General Victor to action on the morning of the 23rd, and we were in readiness to march off the ground at five o'clock, when we were countermanded to our disappointment. The Spanish General Cuesta, it is reported, would not fight on a Sunday. Well, he might be a very good Christian General, but he was no match for the French unless he could take, at any time, any advantage that might occur. This was an opportunity lost, for during the night the French retreated to St Olala, falling back upon their own strength.

On the 24th, Monday, the Spanish General was surprised to find that the French had left their position. He now marched to pursue them and drive them out of Madrid, and fight them wherever he could find them. Sir Arthur explained that the British had no provisions, and that we could not move until these were supplied. But the Spaniard was obstinate, and crossed the river after the French; he was to do great things with the Spanish army since he got the French on the retreat. This day we waited patiently for a supply of biscuit, but none came. In the evening two pounds of beef each man were served out; this kept us cooking most of the night.

On the 25th We advanced to the Alberche and moved a division of cavalry and foot, under command of General Sherbrooke, across the river, to keep communication with the Spaniards and Sir Robert Wilson's division of Portuguese, who were far advanced on the road to Madrid, to our left. This division occupied the position the French had retreated from at Casalegas. We then returned to our old ground, and sent out parties in search of bread or wine, others being sent to gather wheat and peas in the fields. Very hard times these. In the evening our foragers returned, and brought a mule with two skins of good wine and some bread. This was distributed among the company.

News reached us that General Cuesta and his Spaniards were in full pursuit of the enemy as far as Torrejos, and that Marshal Victor had gone on the Toledo road, where he was joined by General Sebastiani and his army. At this place the French, hearing that the British army was still at Talavera, faced about on the poor Spaniards. On the 26th news arrived almost every hour from the Spanish army that they had been attacked and beaten with great loss, and were retreating in confusion. I saw one of our officers who had been as far as St Olala; he stated that the streets of that town were entirely blocked up with the Spanish artillery, bread-wagons, baggage, etc., and that whole regiments were running like a rabble or a mob. We began to hear a cannonading at a distance, rolling nearer to us.

On the 27th the Spaniards began to arrive; they took up the ground on our right, in two lines, and entrenched themselves and made batteries on the high-road leading from the town to the bridge over the Alberche, and planted their heavy cannon in front of a chapel at our right. We expected a general attack, and our line was drawn between the river and the hill, a distance of about two or three miles. General Sherbrooke was called in from Casalegas, and General MacKenzie was stationed with a strong advanced-post at some houses in a wood. I was sent with a working-party to raise a battery on some rising ground among the olive-trees. About two o'clock the French arrived at the side of the Alberche, and opened fire on our advance-guard, fording the river at the same moment. We kept them in check; but from where I was I could see that our people were suffering much, and retiring to take up their position in the line. The working-parties were ordered to stand to their arms, as the shot from the French was coming thick among us. We were then ordered to join our regiments as quickly as possible, and we joined our battalion on the side of the hill to the left of the line.

A dreadful cannonade commenced on the British right, and the enemy attacked the Spaniards with their cavalry, thinking to break their lines and get into the town; but the Dons repulsed them manfully. The firing ceased on the right after dark, when the French had made a charge of infantry without success. From the place where we stood we could see every movement on the plain.

At this time our brigade got a biscuit each man served out, when a cry was heard, "The hill! the hill!" General Stewart called out for the detachments to make for the top of the hill, for he was certain that no regiment could be there so soon as we. Off we ran in the dark, and very dark it was; but the French got on the top of the hill before us, and some of them ran through the battalion, calling out, *"Espanioles, Espanioles,"* and others calling *"Allemands."*

Our officers cried out "Don't fire on the Spaniards."

I and many others jumped to the side to let them pass down the hill, where they were either killed or taken prisoners in our rear. I saw those on the top of the hill by the flashes of their pieces; then we knew who they were; but I and many more of our company were actually in rear of the French for a few moments, and did not know it until they seized some of our men by the collar and were dragging them away prisoners. This opened our eyes, and bayonets and the butts of our firelocks were used with great dexterity a dreadful melee. The 29th Regiment came to our assistance, charged, and kept possession of the top of the hill. This regiment lost a number of men on the highest point of the hill, where the French had a momentary possession, and affairs hung in the balance ere it was decided who should have this key of the position. The enemy tried it a second time, coming round the side of the hill; but as we now knew who they were, to our cost, a well-directed running fire, with a charge, sent them into the valley below, their drums beating a retreat.

General Hill's division arrived, with two guns, after the affair was over, and, I was told, got credit for this hard contest, though really they were dragging their guns about the foot of the hill and did not fire a shot here until next morning. The firing ceased on this point before eleven o'clock; all was silent on the plain long before. Our brigade got into formation as well as it could, with our left to the top joining General Hill; a deep ravine or hollow was to our front. Some other regiments came on the side of the hill and formed a second line, and some guns were posted to the right of our brigade. I believe it was only after nightfall that our Generals found the importance of this post. We got ammunition served out, and had time to count our loss, which was very great. Vedettes were placed a few yards in front, and we sat down in the ranks and watched every movement of the enemy. About one in the morning we could hear and see the French moving their artillery on the other side of the hollow about two hundred yards from us. Some firing commenced; it ran from the left to the right for we could see every flash in the plain below us.

Order was restored, and a deathlike silence reigned among us. The French kindled great fires in rear of their lines. I had a sound sleep for a short time, being one of those who could sleep half an hour or twenty minutes at any time or place and feel myself much refreshed.

When daylight appeared each army gazed on the other and viewed the operations of last night. Round the top of the hill many a red coat lay dead; about thirty yards on the other side the red and blue lay mixed, and a few yards farther, and down to the valley below, they were all blue. The French fired one gun from the centre as a signal for all their line to commence action. Their guns began to pour grapeshot and shell into our lines, and three columns came bearing for the hill.

We were ordered to lie close to the ground, but when the enemy was about fifty yards from us we started to our feet and poured in a volley, then charged with the bayonet, and ran them down into the valley, cheering and firing upon them, for they proved better runners than we. They retreated across the valley to our left, leaving many killed and wounded behind them, we took some ammunition-wagons, from one of which I took two three-pound loaves of bread. This was a noble prize where there were so many hungry men.

We were ordered to pursue no further than the rising ground at the foot of the left side of the hill. They crossed the valley and formed on some rocks on the other side, and threatened to turn our left. Two Spanish battalions were sent over to them, which kept them in check, and they kept up a popping fire at each other most of the day. Our guns on the top and side of the hill kept blazing away upon the French guns and columns within reach.

After the march was over here, we heard some heavy firing down on the plain among the olive-grounds, but from where we now were we could not see what was going on; the 48th Regiment and some others were withdrawn from the hill to the plain. About eleven o'clock the enemy, being baffled in all his attacks upon our lines, withdrew his troops a little. As we did not move to follow them they deliberately piled arms and set about kindling fires and cooking their victuals. A brook ran through the plain; to it both armies went for water as if truce was between us, looking at each other, drinking, and wiping the sweat from their brows, laughing and nodding heads to each other; all thoughts of fighting for the time being forgotten. Water was in great demand by our brigade, and parties were sent off for it; others were sent to bury the dead that lay thick about us, and to assist the wounded to the rear.

Our brigade took up the ground it had quitted in the morning and the 48th and 66th Regiments took up our ground, for we expected the enemy to make another rush for the top of the hill, and in this we were not deceived. About one o'clock the French army was in motion again, and three divisions were on their way to the hill, one on each side, the other to the front. Our guns on the hill opened upon them, but did little execution to what we expected; it was said, "They are the German Legion artillery." The enemy's right division got under shelter of a large house in the valley, where they stood in close column and sent forward their sharpshooters to within a few yards of us.

At this time the British cavalry entered the valley to check the French right. The 23rd and German hussars formed across the valley, and, supported by the heavy dragoons, charged the right division of the enemy. This charge, though nobly executed, had not the effect intended, for the French opened a steady fire upon them, killed and wounded and took many of the 23rd Light Dragoons prisoners, and forced the remainder back on General Anson's heavy brigade, which kept this division of the enemy from advancing any farther.

We stood looking at the affray for a few moments, until General Stewart's brigade was ordered to advance to the top of the hollow, when all the others were ordered to lie close to the ground, as the French had taken up a position with their heads above the rise, and were doing much mischief. We sustained a heavy fire from the enemy's guns on the other side of the hollow; they were making lanes through us, and their musketry attacked us on our flanks. We cleared the enemy from our front and right, but they maintained the heights on the other side; and, as we were lower than they, they punished us severely. All the other troops were brought into action, and the battle raged along the lines from right to left, and nothing could be heard but the long roll of musketry and the thunder of the artillery intermixed. Captain MacPherson of the 35th Regiment, who commanded our company this day, was down, and my right file was taken off by a cannon-shot. William Bowie and John Shewan were killed on my left, and Adam Much lay in the rear, wounded.

About four o'clock I was struck by a musket ball, which grazed my left knee and passed through my right leg about two inches below the cap of the knee. I finished my loading and fired my last shot at the man who wounded me, for I could plainly see him on a height a few yards to my front; I think I should have known him if he had come in my way afterwards. I called out to Sergeant John Gordon that I was wounded; he was the only non-commissioned officer belonging to the regiment I saw at his post. I made along the side of the hill as well as I could, using my firelock as a crutch.

I now looked back at the brigade, and saw it was much cut up. I passed Colonel Alexander Gordon, formerly captain in our regiment, killed; and Brigade-Major Gardener, who had been an active officer in our brigade all morning he and his horse lay dead together; Major Ross, 38th, and Captain Bradley, 28th Light company, (I knew him in the light battalion in Dublin), badly wounded. I stepped over many men lying on the ground here to rise again no more. The shot was tearing up the ground on my left and right, as the French cannon were doing great execution at this time, and their shells had set the cornfields on fire in the plain, and brushwood and long grass were blazing on the sides of the hill; and many wounded men, unable to get away, were burned to death. If I had sat down no doubt the same lot would have been mine, so I kept hopping along until I came to a large white house where many wounded men were waiting to be dressed. Here I

106

found the surgeon of the Gordons, Dr Beattie, who came at once to me and dressed my leg and put a bandage on it. He then gave me a drink of water, and told me I had got it at last. I, smiling, replied, 'Long run the fox, but he is sure to be caught at last.' This made many smile whose bones were sore enough.

I had now time to look about me, and I saw that we were going on in the plain little to our advantage. Some of our guns were drawn to the rear to take up a fresh alignment. Feeling very weak, I took a mouthful of water and a slice of the loaf that I got in the morning, when I found a musket ball in it, which had pierced my haversack and lodged in the loaf. I sincerely returned thanks to God for preserving me in the dangers to which I had been exposed, and gave myself great credit for all I had done. Thus pleased with myself, I got up and hopped along for the town of Talavera.

I trudged along in the rear of the line towards the town with some more men in the same condition, although about this time it seemed rather doubtful whether the French would be there before us. I felt myself getting very weak through loss of blood, and had to make many halts among the olive-trees; and I was vexed to see so many men of different regiments, especially of the King's German Legion, skulking in the rear when they should have been doing their duty in front with their comrades going prowling about with bad intentions I knew by their looks. And as for the Spaniards, some battalions of them had left the field in mobs during the action; not those actually engaged, but those in the second and third lines. This was disgraceful conduct.

I reached the town and sat down on the steps of a door, when a young woman brought me a pitcher of water and vinegar, and many a pull I took of it before I let it out of my hands. I then went to the general hospital, a large convent, where hundreds of men were lying in the courts and passages, and on the stairs. I lay down and put my head on the dead body of a man of the 61st Regiment, and slept amid all the uproar and bustle. I awakened about dark, and got into one of the large rooms. I saw no one I knew but Adam Much of our regiment, who was wounded about the same place as myself. I lay down beside him. We slept soundly until morning, when I was wakened by the surgeons performing their operations, cutting off legs and arms. I found myself stiff and sore. Dr Beattie came and dressed our wounds On the afternoon of the 29th Adam Much's wife found him; this was a joyful meeting, as he was supposed to be killed. I got about two glasses of wine from her, which greatly revived me; this was a glass in need, not to be forgotten.

On the 30th we were carried to the battalion hospital, situated in a church. I got plenty of clean straw, and had one of the steps of the high altar for a pillow, and had some good soup, of which I had much need. Here I learnt the particulars of both armies. The firing was kept up until evening, and we kept our ground and no more on the 28th. Early on the morning of the 29th, when a fresh attack was expected, the French crossed the Alberche and retreated in good order to their old positions.

Thus, although commanded by King Joseph in person, and Marshals Victor and Jourdan, and General Sebastiani, with about forty-eight thousand men, they could make no impression on the British lines, and we were the mainstay of the Spaniards. In this action our loss was very great. Generals MacKenzie and Langworth were killed in the field. According to a statement which I saw, the number of killed and wounded was: officers, three hundred and thirty-seven; sergeants, two hundred and eight; drummers, twenty-nine; rank and file, four thousand eight hundred and ninety-two a total of five thousand four hundred and sixty-six. Of the first battalion of detachments there were above three hundred men killed and wounded. Our company had forty-eight men in the field, of whom six were killed and twenty-four wounded.

CHAPTER 4

The Fruits of Victory

The French army must have suffered much more than we did; we may safely add one-half more. Some cannon fell into our hands, with a very few prisoners. The Spanish loss was about one thousand two hundred killed and wounded; what they had missing no one could tell, as they went off to the rear in droves. Thus we may say a great battle was fought or trial of strength made for no important end what- ever. The day after all this was over, a light brigade, three thousand strong, and a troop of horse artillery arrived from Lisbon under Brigadier-General Crawford. I suppose the French had got intelligence of this, which made them draw off and put the river Alberche betwixt us, and some despatches from General Jourdan fell into our hands, telling Marshal Soult to march from Salamanca speedily by the Puerta del Banos and Placencia, there to be joined by the divisions under Ney and Mortier, and then fall on the rear of the British army. This opened our eyes. There was only one way of avoiding this snare, and that was to retreat immediately across the Tagus by the bridge of Arzobispo, and take up a defensive position where provisions could be got for the army. I never received any correct intelligence of our army after the retreat, not so much even as a flying report.

On the 31st July, Colonel Bunbury, commanding our battalion, got bread and *aguardiente*, which he divided himself among the wounded men in hospital. He expressed his satisfaction with our behaviour in the different actions in which he had had the honour to command us; and Sir Arthur, he said, had expressed his thanks to the first battalion of detachments for their bravery and good conduct in the night attack upon the hill and during the whole of the 28th, and he would not fail to represent it to His Majesty. Next day he sent a doubloon's worth of bread and two skins of wine for the use of the wounded. This was of more benefit to us than the fine speech he made yesterday, and was a great relief to every man in the hospital. He ordered all the battalion to be paid to 24th July the last money I received for many a day; and he waited in the hospital until he saw the wounded men get their money, and was exceedingly attentive to us as far as lay in his power. Large parties of Spaniards were sent to gather the dead men and horses into heaps and burn them, for fear of causing a plague about the town.

On the 2nd of August all the British troops marched off by daybreak we thought to attack the enemy; but, to our horror, we found they had retreated, leaving us wounded men in a dreadful condition, without provisions, only a few surgeons, little medicine, and no attendants. About twelve o'clock Dr Beattie came in and desired every man that was able to make the best of his way after the army, for he expected the French in the town in a few hours. This caused a great consternation among us. I had been very cheery in the morning, but this made me change my tune. Spanish officers came through the church among us, bringing in mules and asses for those that were able to ride. Many tried to leave the place, but had to return before night; and many were obliged to lie down in the fields who never rose again.

Sergeant MacBean got a mule for himself and me, but by this time I could neither sit nor stand, my wound was so bad and my leg swollen. He got on and pranced down the centre of the church like a mounted hussar. I bade him God speed and asked him to tell my comrades if ever he reached the regiment where he had left me. When it was growing dark, who should come into the church, crawling on all-fours, but Sergeant MacBean! He crept in among the straw beside me, and we kept together until our wounds were healed over. So we were obliged to content ourselves and remain at the mercy of the French.

There were about thirty French wounded men in the church, and well they could observe what was going on. They were in great terror for the Spaniards. Some of them got red coats, caps, Highland bonnets, etc., that they might pass for British. One tall, fine looking man got on a kilt, hose, and big coat. He was wounded in the shoulder, but could make good use of his legs, and was water-carrier for all about our corner, and was ready to help every one; he would answer to no name but Grenadier *"Sansculotte."*

On the 4th the Spanish troops left the town, and took their own wounded with them, but none of the British, who were left in a very helpless condition, more especially those belonging to our battalion, as we had nobody to take charge or yet attend us. I certainly blame Dr Beattie for this, as other corps left their assistant-surgeon, orderlies, hospital sergeant etc., while we were destitute of any assistance. On the 5th John Murray, who had been in the general hospital with the fever, came and found us in this helpless condition; and, poor fellow, although weak himself, yet having the use of his limbs, he did all he could to make us comfortable. He got us removed to the general hospital, a large convent in a fine airy situation. We stationed ourselves in one of the passages on the second floor, and here we were for many a day beside some men of the 2nd battalion 24th Regiment. There were only four of our regiment left here that we knew of namely, Sergeant Alexander MacBean, Donald Johnston, John Murray and myself. Murray recovered strength rapidly, and was made cook in the hospital; yet whenever his time permitted he gave us all the attention in his power. We were visited frequently by the general doctor, Higgins, who ordered us to dress each other's wounds morning and evening.

On the 6th the French entered the town and carried on a regular system of plunder, breaking open every shut door they found, and every article that was of value to them was carried off. A great quantity of provisions found hidden in the houses of the town from our armies was now distributed with a liberal hand by the French soldiers who did not forget their English enemies. I got a mattress and a set of red window curtains, which served me as blankets until I entered France. The indefatigable John Murray let us want for nothing he could get; he brought us soap, linen to dress our wounds, etc. The French mounted a guard over this large convent, as much as to say, "You are prisoners of war." All who were able had liberty to go out and in through the day, and Marshal Victor gave strict orders to use us civilly, and not to take any article from us, but to purchase anything we had to dispose of. For a few days our hospital was crowded from morning to night with French soldiers come to get a sight of the English wounded, and some to purchase shoes, which were in great demand. I sold a new pair for a dollar, not to be troubled any more, for I saw some taking them by force, and I remembered the order given to some of the British at Braga, to strip every French prisoner they saw with a good pair of shoes.

On 7th August we got rations from the French, three pounds of coarse bread for every eight men, and a very small quantity of beef to make soup (*boullion*, as they called it), without salt or vegetables. The French got a regular market established in the town, which was more than the British or Spaniards could do while they had command of it; and it surprised us much that the people of the country would hide stores of provisions from their own army and ours, who were willing to pay ready-money for them. However, the French are good foragers, and I have seen at times much good come out of intended evil. Plenty of white bread, fruit, wines, etc., were brought into the market and sold for ready money.

On 15th August we were alarmed by the French artillery firing, we thought it to be some attack; but it turned out to be the birthday of the French Emperor. They fired at daybreak, midday, and sunset. On the 24th fever got in amongst us and swept away great numbers, especially men who had limbs amputated or were wounded, so as to be unable to attend to themselves; for men get selfish in the midst of misery, and if a man could not help himself, alas for him! About this time a wagon attended every morning to take away the dead. The driver of this wagon I shall never forget. He was a very tall man in the dress of a French prisoner, with long black beard and moustaches an ugly man. He stood in the middle of the passages and bawled out, making the place ring again, *'Combien de mort Anglais le jour?'* which is nearly, 'How many dead Englishmen today?' If there were none he would shrug his shoulders and mutter a curse; if one or more he seemed happy, saying *'Bon!'* (Good). Then the wretch would seize the dead by the ankles and drag him off to his wagon. I heard he got a franc for every corpse he took out of the convent.

According to report, there were two thousand six hundred British left here; but we were getting thinned rapidly by death and desertions. The French caused a general muster to be made, as some of our people had been caught and brought back while trying to make their escape. All who could walk were mustered and forty cartloads of wounded were sent off to Madrid; this gave us more room, but we were more strictly looked after by the French. My leg and thigh swelled to an alarming extent. The general doctor and Dr Taylor of the Sixty-sixth Regiment were for cutting it off; but to this I objected, and told them I might as well go to the grave with two legs as one.

I continued poulticing the wound with the bread that should have gone into my belly, and I suffered great pain. But I was relieved in an extraordinary manner. One night after it was dark a French drummer was pursuing a woman belonging to the Twenty-fourth Regiment in full flight along the passage, when she fell right on my wounded leg. I roared out, the woman shrieked, and the drummer, thinking he was to be attacked, drew his sword and went off cursing. I was in great distress and in a high fever all night; but next morning, on dressing my wound, seven small pieces of bone came out of it, some of them about the size of the teeth of a dressing-comb, and a piece of my trousers that had been driven in by the ball. From this time I mended every day. I was well attended by Sergeant MacBean, who was wounded in the hip which had now healed, and he could limp about on a stick, bring water, wash our linen, etc.; but one day he fell in the cook-house, and had to take to his bed, to my great loss and his own. However, this accident was fortunate for him, for his wound broke out afresh, and two pieces of his trousers were discharged. In a few days he was on his feet again, and he cut me some young olive-trees to make me a pair of crutches, and did everything in his power to get me mounted on these.

My wound was skinned over on the 2nd of October, two months after I received it, and I began to look forward a little, for some weeks I had not expected to leave the convent but by the help of Combien de mart, the French wagoner. My first start out of doors was to the river Tagus, which ran past the foot of the garden, to wash my shirts. I sat in the sun till I got sick, and had to keep my bed with a kind of fever and ague, which went through amongst us.

On the 5th November, Sunday, the hospital was visited by Marshal Mortier and his staff. He was a tall, stout man, with a star on his breast. He told us he was sorry it was not in his power to supply us with many things we stood in need of, but while bread was to be got for his own troops we should be first served. He said the French had used us better than our own army had done, in leaving us in the state they found us; for the Spaniards, being our friends, could have provided the means of transporting the wounded if our commanders chose; but instead of this we had been left a burden to the French army. He also told us that many British had made their escape; but some had been shot, and if any of us were caught in future a mile from the town we might expect to be served in the same manner. All this he said in English, and left, it is said, one hundred and sixty doubloons to purchase wine, rice, etc., for the use of the hospital. I believe it was entrusted to bad hands, and not half of it was expended in the use it was intended for.

On the 7th November the French seemed in a bustle: drums beating, cannons driven to and fro, and planted in position on the roads leading from the town and by the riverside. A battery had been built at the end of the bridge across the Tagus, which had been repaired; but now the planks of the centre arch were removed and the French stores packed up. On our going for rations the commissary told us to *reste tranquille*, and the Spaniards would serve us out tomorrow. The Spanish troops remained in sight all day, and we thought they meant to attack the town and set us at liberty; but no such thing. The French marched out at night; we could see the fires of both armies, and supposed the French meant to begin the attack in the morning. But the Spaniards moved off; the French repaired the bridge in quick time, and sent troops after them, and more arrived from Madrid. Sergeant MacBean and many others resolved to make their escape; as the Spaniards were in the neighbourhood, they thought they might fall in with them before long.

On the evening of the 9th MacBean took leave of me for the second time. I gave him a loaf of bread, a small map of the country, and a letter to my mother. I never was more vexed in parting from any man, yet I advised him to start, he being married and a persevering man, and likely to succeed in anything he took in hand. Next day I got out to market and bought some bread and grapes, etc., and found my money getting very small; yet I never spent money to such good purpose as at Talavera. There seemed to be a blessing in it, and I often had something extra when feeling badly.

The French General discovered that many of our men had escaped since the Spanish troops came near. Early on the morning of the 12th, without previous notice, all the British officers, doctors, and every man that was expected to live were turned out to the square, and were put on bullock-carts, and driven out of the town on the road to Madrid. We crossed the well-contested plain and the river Alberche, and saw many dead men's bones picked bare on both sides of the bridge, which was now repaired. Reached St Olala after it was dark; this town was nearly deserted by its inhabitants. The French guard were very kind to our wounded men, carrying those unable to walk from the carts into some stables, with their baggage, etc. Those troops that had fought in the field with us were always the kindest and readiest to assist us; when we had a guard of young conscripts they were very troublesome to every one.

13th. To Ventas. It was dark before we reached it, although the French soldiers pricked the bullocks with their bayonets to get the carts on. This is a very slow method of travelling, and we all were very tired sitting huddled on the carts. Two of our people died on this day's march through fatigue and want of sustenance. We passed through a dreary, uncultivated country, with no houses between the stages, and no food could be got. In the afternoon we saw from a height the spires and part of the ancient city of Toledo, across an uncultivated plain to our right.

14th. To Pitho, a village within three leagues of the capital. The country begins to be better cultivated and more sheltered with trees, etc.; we had passed over but a barren waste since we crossed the Alberche.

15th. Started before daylight to get early into the city. The French soldiers seemed very happy to get there, and so were we poor wounded prisoners; although we knew not what our condition was to be, we knew it could not be worse than it had been. We viewed the majestic appearance of the city, with its fine spires, domes, and churches, with the sun shining brilliantly upon them, as we approached it from the west, there being no hill to hide it from our view. The French cavalry was quartered in all the villages along the road, and sentries were placed on the tops of some or the churches and high houses to observe the plain country, for fear of being surprised by the Spaniards.

We crossed a shallow river by a stone bridge on the west side of the city. There we saw hundreds of women washing on both sides of the river as far as we could see; each dame on her knees with a board in front of her, rubbing and washing, and singing cheerily. A hardy race of ladies, I could see from their countenances; they sympathised much with us in our distress. We passed some avenues of trees up to the city, which is surrounded by an earthen wall, with gates and a strong guard of French at each entrance. We halted. Notice of our arrival was sent to the commandant, who ordered us round to the Puerta del Sol, a spacious square with many streets leading from it. Crowds of people came round, asking when and where we were taken, and giving us bits of bread, money, etc., until the French soldiers drove them off with the butts of their firelocks. We were lodged for the night in the great military hospital. Each man received a small measure of wine and a piece of bread, of which we had much need. We thought the first stage of our misery was over.

A British Prisoner
in France

CHAPTER 1

In the Sierras

At Madrid, after the battle of Solanese, we had good accommodation, each patient having a bed and blanket and good provisions of white bread, 1lb. of beef with soup, and a pint of wine twice a day. We rejoiced to find such good rations after keeping Lent so long. We found here some of the first parties sent from Talavera looking clean and well. On the 18th November all that had no open wounds were examined by a French doctor in order to be forwarded to France, and about 200 were picked out and sent to the Retire, a place in the east part of the city, nigh the palace.

This place was enclosed with stockades, and the French were busy erecting batteries making it into a fortification, as it stands on a commanding situation; all houses in the way were taken down, and parties of the inhabitants were daily at work upon the batteries, redoubts, etc. We prisoners were lodged in the Riding School, a shocking dirty place to put either man or beast into, and the fever soon broke out amongst us. In front of us was the Grand Square or Parade, where guards and all duties were mounted, and where King Joseph and some of the French Marshals usually attended.

A party of Spaniards taken prisoners only a few leagues from the city was brought here; a sergeant-major and an intelligent lad of about sixteen assured us we would be relieved in three or four days, as some large Spanish armies were advancing on the city. This we believed, as the French seemed in a bustle. On the 22nd I and some others having the fever were sent in two carts back to the hospital. The inhabitants were exceedingly kind to the British wounded while passing through the streets, giving them money, shirts, and shoes, unperceived by the French.

On the 28th, before daylight, a heavy cannonading began on the east of the city. This made us think the Spanish armies were attacking the French and that we would all be speedily relieved as we knew there were not many French troops in town; but to our mortification we found it to be the celebration of the fact that King Joseph and the French had now been a year in possession of Madrid. Some of the inhabitants thought it was a trick to see if any of them would turn out and the French dragoons were ready to fall upon them.

On 4th December arrived sixty wagons loaded with Spanish soldiers wounded at the battle of Ocana where the French destroyed the army that was to take Madrid, and thousands of prisoners were marched past the hospital on their way to France, very miserable looking soldiers indeed. All hopes of our being relieved were now sunk in despair, until a general exchange or the end of the war.

I continued very bad and there was no man in the fever ward I had ever seen before, and the Spanish orderly men would rather play cards than give assistance to anybody. One night I crawled out of my bed to a window where stood a large earthen jar with water. I brought it to one side to get some, when down it came upon me on the floor, and there I lay on the bricks in a fine cold bath until the orderly man came. He with many damns and curses lifted me up and heaved me into bed, making my bones crack again all for a thing I could not help. For ten days after I was unable to move about, then I was removed out of the fever ward, a place where I expected death and prayed to God fervently to receive my soul, for I had no desire or inclination to live. But it pleased the Lord to prolong my days when numbers were cut off around me.

Christmas Day was ushered in with the ringing of bells from all the churches in the city, and I believe no town in Europe has so many places of worship as Madrid. I now began to walk about and had plenty of room for exercise in the galleries and passages of this large building, which is for South America what our East India house in London is for India. It was called by the French the Military Hospital of St Francis, and no place in Madrid could have better accommodation for the sick, with a fine free air. I soon recovered strength, and was often sent out into the town; this was by the favour of a Spanish orderly man named Antonio, for whom I sold tobacco. By this I made a little money to help me on my journey to France.

The fine weather set in on Tuesday 20th February 1810, and thirty-seven British cripples were to have carts and join some French officers and 200 Spanish prisoners. This day I had a fine view of Madrid. We having only a French grenadier sergeant in charge of us, and being in number thirty-seven, and all cripples, halted where we thought proper, and examined any curiosities.

We passed through many fine streets and squares, and saw many tradesmen working in the streets in front of their shops. We were stopped by an old Scotch lady opposite her house; she gave us each a glass of wine and a piece of bread and about two pence. in money; the French sergeant got a double allowance. Passed through the Plaza Major, one of the finest squares I saw in the city; it has many fine buildings, generally of brick, with the under stories strongly stanchioned with iron bars, which gives them the appearance of prisons. This is also a public market place. Our sergeant gave us leave to see a Spanish execution, and he drove the Spaniards out of the way with many hard names to let his British friends have a front view. The man was on the scaffold with some friars about him in a praying posture. He was then seated on a stool with a post behind him, when his neck was squeezed with a cord to the post until he was choked.

On the east side of the town we passed along some fine walks shaded with trees and some fountains of water representing Neptune in his chariot drawn by horses with streams of water issuing from their mouths; in other parts of the walks were figures of men, women, fishes, etc., all spouting water. Passed in front of the Palace, two stories high on a rising ground, and entered the Retiro now a complete French garrison. We were put into a room where I had a very dirty billet.

On the 21st we were put into bullock carts and bade *adieu* to Madrid with all its fine steeples and churches and fountains, and above all, its kind inhabitants, who I believe used the British wounded as well as they durst for fear of the French. We were escorted by about 200 French, a skeleton regiment going to France to be filled up. A major commanded who had lost all his baggage at Oporto when the British entered. He did all he could to make us comfortable. I being the best at speaking French of our party, he and I kept up conversation, so as to be understood, in French, Spanish, and English all mixed together.

We crossed the river Manzanares which half winds round the city, and halted at Las Rozas, where we were crammed into stables, the town being full of troops. Indeed every village had French in it and some of the houses were fortified as barracks, for they were obliged to protect the roads to keep open communication with France, and could only move from place to place in large bodies, for fear of the Spaniards attacking them, which they often did. Between all the contending parties the country was in a very unsettled state.

On the 22nd we saw the Escurial, a stately palace at the foot of the hills about half a league from us to the left of the road; the sun shining bright upon it at the time gave it a grand appearance. There is a large extent of deer parks surrounded with high walls on the plain.

We began to ascend the mountains the Sierra de Guadarrama, which were covered with trees, and I saw the bones of many Spaniards belonging to former parties of prisoners who had been shot by the French for those sick or lame who were unable to keep up were instantly shot without being given an opportunity or offering up a prayer for their souls. Many of their bodies were picked bare by the wolves and birds, eagles, etc., which inhabit these mountains. We were obliged to walk here as the bullocks had enough to do, in pulling up the empty carts, to keep pace with the party. The French kept us as close together as they could; notwithstanding this some of the Spaniards at one of the zigzag turns of the road made a rush into the wood and got clear off. The French halted the party and kept firing after them but to no end; they then beat unmercifully with the butts of their firelocks some of those who remained. To this bad usage the Spaniards patiently submitted; but no wonder that retaliation came upon the French in their own evil day.

We reached the top and had a splendid view of the plain country on both sides of the mountains. The French had a battery and some works in the principal passes, with men in huts a very cold position, as the snow lay not far from them. Halted at about eleven o'clock at night at a small village called Ortar, and got a snug room to ourselves.

On the 23rd we passed a royal palace at the foot of this great range of mountains, called Ildefonso. We halted while the French officers went to it (it lay a little to the left, off the road) and got breakfast. Came to Segovia, a fine town surrounded by a wall with turrets in the Moorish style, with a castle, etc. It lies between two valleys with streams of water. A brigade of Germans in the French service was doing duty here. There is an ancient aqueduct here said to have been built by the Romans which conducts water over the river Frio and a deep valley into the town. The arches are exceedingly high, built without lime or cement. The inhabitants were kind to us: we were quartered in a convent. Many of our Spaniards got into hospital here. 24th to Santa Maria. This village was *palisadoed*, and we entered by a drawbridge into the French barracks; most of their stations were done in the same manner. Here some Spanish officers joined our party.

Since we passed the mountains that divide the Old and New Castiles the country is of a wild nature, bare and uncultivated, 25th, to Baladosphe, a village. 26th, to Baldeer. Here lay a Dutch regiment which had been charged at Talavera by the 23rd Dragoons: they showed us many of the appointments of that regiment. 27th, passed a long sandy plain among fir trees; crossed a stone bridge over the Douro, which river has here a very different appearance. The French have some very strong works here to defend the passage of the river. There had been a large village here but it is now burnt down and in ruins. We met two regiments of Dutch on the road some of their men hailed us in good English.

There was also a regiment of Polish Lancers, formidable looking men, the first I had seen, but I met many afterwards.

We arrived at Valladolid, which stands in the midst of a fertile plain and is watered by two small rivers. The first thing that presented itself to us at the gate was the body of a Spaniard nailed high up on the wall in the same manner and attitude in which he was taken, with his guns beside him. I was told he had been a chief of brigands and had murdered some French soldiers in a cruel manner. The Spanish officers sighed and hung their heads as they passed.

A guard of French cavalry turned out as we passed on to the market place where stood the French park of artillery some very heavy battering cannon and mortars drawn up in three lines. This place is called El Campo and is surrounded by a number of convents many of them converted into barracks for the French, as a division of their army lay here at this time. We passed another fine square with good buildings having *piazzas* all round and many good shops. The houses are more regularly built here than in Madrid being about four stories high with iron balconies gilded, which look well when the sun shines on them. There is a large cathedral, a university, and many churches with hospitals. In the streets are many fountains and fine gardens within the wall. This is the best looking city I have seen in Spain and the inhabitants look very respectable in a time like this when the country is in such a state of confusion.

We were quartered in an old convent on the south side of the city, facing the open country. Our rations here were scanty, but we had liberty to purchase. Bread was our only demand; it was for sale for about 3d. for a 4lb loaf of the finest flour. We got wine clear as distilled water very cheap.

The army of Portugal consisting of about thirty thousand men were drawn up on the plain, to be reviewed by Marshal Massena and General Jounot. We had a fine view of them from the roof of the convent, where we were permitted to go by the French commandant, who pointed out

129

to us the Generals and the movements of the army. He was an old wounded veteran and was rejoiced to see them, exclaiming *'Bon!'* or *'Bravo!'* at every change of position. While here three men of a party of British which had arrived before us were shot while attempting to escape.

We remained at Valladolid until 22nd March when at daybreak a party of us of twenty men and six women, British, and about a hundred Spanish were turned out without rations and delivered over to a captain who was to escort them. He was told to shoot any man that fell behind or that attempted to escape. But the captain was a humane man and got the British into artillery wagons; we went six leagues this day.

CHAPTER 2
L'Amor de Dieu

Being very hungry and seeing a French soldier with more bread than he could make use of I asked him to sell me some. This he would not do but gave me a large piece for *'L'amor de Dieu.'* This was the first charity I received in my life and from an enemy too. The good man certainly thought I had need of it and he was right. I thought much of his kindness especially as he had carried the bread so many miles on his back. Halted at Bertavilla where we were lodged in a chapel; here we got plenty of bread and soup. 23rd, met some heavy cannon and ordnance stores with an escort of French cavalry. Halted at Pallanzuela which lies low between two rivers; here we were joined by a party of the Guards (British wounded) who had been detained all winter at Palencia where they were fed by the inhabitants like fighting cocks. When they began to make their escape the French hurried them off.

24th, to Mazula. This day we were put in alarm by a body of Spaniards who came down the hill on our left and showed as if they meant to attack the party. The French drums beat to arms, the advance and rear guards closed; a guard was left with the prisoners with orders to fire if any one offered to move, and a party was sent forward to bring the Spaniards to action, but they scampered up the sides of the hills. 25th, to Pamplige. We were now getting into a better cultivated country, villages more plentiful and good roads.

26th, reached Burgos, the most thriving town I have seen in Spain. But for the presence of the French troops who had raised some works and fortified the Castle, which commands the town, there was no sign of war here. We crossed the bridge over the river; a guard of gendarmes was stationed here, and I saw some Mamelukes riding after some of the French generals as orderlies, but they were not to be compared with the fine looking fellows I saw in Egypt. Here also I saw many British soldiers who had volunteered into the French service. We had a fine clean room in the centre of the city and were allowed port liberty. There is a large cathedral with a fine spire of curious workmanship. The streets are broad, and level by the river side; there are many good shops and everyone seemed to be employed.

We halted here on the 27th, and some gentlemen of the town came among us and gave us money telling us it was raised by the inhabitants for the British wounded. On the 28th we were put into bullock carts and got on a good road planted with trees on each side many or them being cherry trees in full blossom. An Irish captain had charge of us. He told us his name was Hussey from Sligo. He said he had been out with the "Boys" in the United Cause and his heart warmed to see us; he gave us a dollar to buy wine, and said he liked the French service very well.

We came to Birbeisca which lies in a hollow; a brook runs through the centre of it; the 3rd French regiment was doing duty here. 29th to Miranda de Elbro having a castle on the hill and many additional works made lately by the French to guard the pass where the road passes through this range of hills. Some friars brought us a large mess of boiled beans which went down very sweetly. 30th to Vit-

132

toria a fine town enclosed by a kind of wall; houses much scattered, gardens inside the walls. The Irish brigade in the French service were on duty here; they came among us looking for volunteers but got none. 31st halted; being Sunday some of our women went begging to the chapel doors and got much money and were soon the worse of liquor and kept rioting and disturbing the party and fighting with their husbands, etc. It is a great pity such vagabonds should be allowed to go abroad with the army.

On the 1st April we first got an escort of gendarmes which was always continued afterwards. Crossed the river Zadona and began to ascend the Pyrenees through a fine fertile country; the sides of the hills covered with wood. This day was very wet and some of our Spaniards got clear off and were not missed until night. We passed through many villages; everything seemed here to be in a state of prosperity. Halted all night at Salvatierra a fine village. 2nd to Villafranca. This day we passed on our right some very high mountains capped with snow; rain on the hills and the sun very hot in the valleys. On the 3rd, we came to Tolosa, a large town. We passed by a stately bridge over a brawling river that comes down from the mountains. In the main street there are boards shelving from each side to throw the rain into the centre. On the sides you can walk dry. The crowd that had collected and the French guards kept us poor prisoners right in the middle where the rain poured on us from neck to heel. I always rejoiced to see our faithful allies the Spaniards do a clean thing. Between twenty and thirty of them made their escape, some into shops, others mixed with the crowd. The French cursed them but being wet and tired gave themselves no further trouble. We were quartered in a chapel. The French had their barracks fortified. 4th, halted; many troops passed here on their way into Spain. 5th, to Audoin. Passed many fine villages; ironworks, water mills, etc., seemed all busy. A battalion of French marines lay here and came to see if any of us would enter the service.

Some American captains whose vessels lay at Sebastian gave us sixpence each: this was very good of Jonathan. 6th, saw St Sebastian off the road to our left; it has a fortified appearance from the heights. Saw some British gun brigs cruising out at sea, we rejoiced to see salt water and British war vessels again. As this was the boundary between Spain and France the French escort had some brandy shouting out 'Vive l'Empereur! Vive la France!' They then handed round the bottle to the British, who emptied it without a 'Vive ' but we felt happy at being on French soil without knowing the reason of our being so.

Came to St Jean de Luz the first town in France. The inhabitants were very kind to us and many young women came among us selling brandy. I got more cheerful here than I had been for ten months before and sold my blanket which I had carried until it was becoming a nuisance; these Frenchwomen were disposed to buy any article we had to dispose of. 7th, to Bayonne a regularly fortified town with a deep river and many ships. We were lodged in the citadel, a very strong place and had the liberty of the courtyard. Here was a gang of convicts in chains with a shot or two dragging after them. These men are made to work on the batteries etc., for a number of years according to the nature of their offences.

On the walls of the fencing were cut in stone the names of some British sailors taken in 1756 and 1760. The Spaniards got money, bread, and beef from Prince Ferdinand but no rations for the British; we were obliged to our faithful allies who gave us a share of their mess. 8th, halted. A man came from the town to see how many were of us; I made out a list of our names and regiments: we got shirts, shoes and trousers; some of our party had much need of them.

CHAPTER 3

The Road to Briancon

On the 9th we marched through the town. Most of the houses look very old and stand with their gables to the streets. Crossed the river by a drawbridge and parted with the Spaniards, who went another road. We expected to embark in boats for Bordeaux but in this we were disappointed. We were marched off by a gendarme who let us walk as we pleased to a village called Parade. 10th, got into transport carts to Orthes, and were put into the Nun's hospital, where those Sisters of Charity attended us and gave us the best of rations, wine, etc. 11th, halted.

12th, to Lescar Hospital. Here we found about seventy or eighty British who had been here for two months. About half of these marched, leaving the remainder and sixty Spaniards, who were in a most filthy state with the itch. Their skin was black, rising in scales like that of a fish; I pitied the poor fellows they were very loathsome to look upon. We had good clean bedding and our rations were good but scanty I wrote a letter to the commissary at Pau, who sent us an order to march after being here for a month.

Thursday, 10th May, we came into Pau, and were met by the Commandant, a very pleasant old gentleman. He told us it was for our good he had kept us in hospital for he was certain we were better there than in our depot; this we afterwards found to be true. He conducted us to the promenade and served us with shirts and shoes, and told us to take care of them, for it would be a long time before we would get any more. We got five *sous* and 1lb. of ration bread every day on the march afterwards. Marched to Tarbes; it was late before we got in. This is a fine large town. Halted here on the 11th, had a good room and full liberty. The Freemasons among us got five francs apiece and in every town where there was a lodge relief was given more or less: a fine thing to be a Mason in France! 12th, got transport wagons to Rabastens; 13th, Miranda; 14th, halt; 15th at Auch, halted in the Grand Square. The inhabitants used us very kindly and gave us bread, money, and wine until half of the party was speaking loud.

This is a beautiful tract of country, well cultivated. Nature is bountiful in her productions here. We passed through to Toulouse which is an ancient city the capital of a fertile province. The soil is very rich and I have seen fields with heavy crops of wheat among rows of large fruit trees and vines at the same time, warped along from tree to tree; this had a beautiful appearance. Here is the river Garonne which is navigable to Bordeaux, and a canal connects the town with the Mediterranean. We crossed the river by a stone bridge; there are some fine level streets and some good buildings in and about the principal square. Provisions of all kinds are very cheap; wine is sold for three or four *sous* a bottle, and brandy for twelve *sous*.

We were quartered in the jail and used but indifferently, for in most of the large towns prisoners of war were strictly looked after. A gentleman waited upon us and told us an exchange of prisoners was going on between the two countries, and that a Mr MacKenzie had come from England to make arrangements. This put us in agitation lest we

136

should not arrive at our depot in time. The gentleman left us some money. We went on to Villefranche: and marched on a long causeway for about six post leagues.

On the 21st we came to Castelnaudary and were put into another dirty jail. It being dark they sold us soup made of snails, and good well seasoned soup it was. Some of our people made a row about it; the French folk just laughed at us. I thought it was composed of livers or lights, and lay down and slept. At this place there is a trade in silk, and here begins the rearing of silkworms, with paper windows, and mulberry trees whose leaves are stripped to feed the silkworms.

On the 22nd we reached Carcassonne, an ancient walled town. A regiment of Spaniards was doing duty here and seemed very happy in the French service. There is an old town and a new separated by the river. 23rd Leanill. Narbonne, a large fortified town in a deep valley among hills has a very ancient appearance: the Grand Canal comes through here many boats passing and re-passing. 25th, to Beziers, a large walled town. In the centre of the principal square is a statue of a Captain Peire who defended the city against the British in days of yore. Monsieur pointed this out to our party in a very *gasconading* manner. This town stands in a well cultivated country, the vineyards on the slopes of the rising ground. We could see the Mediterranean with its gentle waves within a couple of miles of us. On the 26th we halted, some nuns or Sisters of Charity came among us, an elderly lady said prayers and gave us bread and wine.

On the 27th we were joined by some Spanish officers three of whom, a colonel and two captains, were in chains having attempted to escape. Seven British and some sailors who had deserted from the French fleet at Toulon also joined us. These sailors got us all into trouble. As we were passing a wood in sight of the sea, the

French tars with a knowing wink and a nod to the British jerked up their trousers sailor fashion and started off. The gendarmes raised a hue and cry and one raised his carbine to fire when out fell the flint. At this we burst into a roar of laughter. The gendarme then turned on us and punished some of us with the butt of his carbine, but the sailors got clear off.

We came to Meze, a town by the seaside: here the gendarmes got us closely locked up. 28th we were badly used by that wicked gendarme; he made one of our party march all day with thumbscrews on for shaking his fist at him, yet I had some sympathy for the gendarme, for I knew myself what it was to lose prisoners. Saw some of our cruisers off the coast, and no doubt we wished ourselves on board. To Poussan; 29th Montpellier. I can say little about this city for I did not see much of it. The air is said to be purer and less scorching than in the surrounding country. It stands on the slope of a hill where you have the great plain between you and the Pyrenees and the Mediterranean, as far as the eye can reach. There are some good stone buildings broad streets and walks shaded with trees, with statues and fountains. Distance from the sea five miles. But for all the fine balmy air of this place it was ordered that we should have none of it at this time, for our officious gendarme reported us as being the occasion of his losing the sailors, and we were locked up in a dungeon in the citadel outside the town until the 31st, when we were glad to see daylight again. Crossed a beautiful country to Lunel.

On 1st June we reached Nimes, an ancient city. On entering there is a Roman amphitheatre which has stood the test of time with little damage. There are three or four rows of arches one above another, some at the bottom are converted into shops; also a large aqueduct called Pont de Font, consisting of three rows of arches said to be above 100 feet high across the river; a citadel with bastions to keep the inhabitants in order, they being chiefly Protestants: the chief trade here is in silk stockings.

At St Esprit we crossed the rapid river Rhone over a stone bridge of thirty arches. We passed through a pleasant country, the Rhone to our left and the roadsides planted with mulberry, cherry and chestnut trees. A regiment of Portuguese was doing duty at Montetimait. We reached Valence, formerly a walled town. There was a large depot for Spaniards at this place. They were allowed to work about the country. We had the liberty of the town. The Spanish officers treated us as well as we could expect, considering their means. On the 9th we arrived at Tain, where we were quartered in a hospital for lunatics, 10th St Marcellin Italian regiment was doing duty here. The chief business in this town is the rearing of silkworms, and the houses have a nasty close smell with them; all the houses about this quarter have paper windows, which give them a disreputable appearance.

On the 11th to Grenoble, capital of the Province of Dauphiny, situated at the entrance of the mountains, a fortified place. Many troops were in the town and we saw some of the Spaniards who had marched on the road with us doing duty in the French service. Provisions are very cheap here. There are some excellent stone buildings and a large square with a fountain throwing water many feet high. Over the archway of the main gate are the words, in large letters, *Port de France*, and over the doors of many houses in the principal streets were the words *'Liberte et Egalite.'* We were quartered in barracks in the citadel. Halted here on 12th and 13th.

On the 14th we entered the mountains; the valleys are well cultivated and the corn harvest was almost over; came to Sombero. On the 16th at St Bonnet, all villages beside a brawling stream rushing down from among the hills, 17th to Gap. Here our women six in number, were sent back to go to England, they carried a letter from every man in the party. This is a fine little town to be in this part of the country, 18th, met a large party of British who had volunteered out of the depot into the Irish brigade in the French service. Halted at a village, Savines. 19th, Embrun, a fortified town. 20th, Largentiere: here the Germans left us to go to Mont Dauphine, a strong fort in one of the passes leading into Italy, a depot for all foreigners taken under the British flag. 21st, met some officers of the Maltese regiment who had been taken in Italy. They gave us each fifteen *sous* a very handsome present in these times of poverty and charged us not to volunteer into the French service, as we would all be exchanged in a few weeks. This was hope for us. We travelled along a very wild road this day, with streams of water rushing down the hills. Reached Briancon.

CHAPTER 4

The Terrible Condition
of Many Prisoners

We were taken into the Governor's office to give our descriptions, our names, the regiments or ships we belonged to, when and where taken, father's and mother's names, when and where born, etc. On coming out we were beset with those harpies of the Irish Brigade, Captain Reilly and Sergeant-Major Dwyer, offering us brandy and telling us all the evils of a French prison; they got three of our party to join them.

Briancon is the last town in France on the principal road to Italy. It lies in one of the passes among the mountains and is very strong both by nature and art. It is surrounded by a single wall. The streets are narrow and steep; the best buildings are the barracks and stores and a church with two steeples. It lies under the Grand Fort or Citadel called les Trois Tetes from which it is separated by a small river called Durance (well named, thought I) over which is a lofty bridge. This bridge, it is said, is the highest in Europe above the sea level: there is a brass plate on it with an inscription stating that it was built in the time of Louis the 14th. The road goes zigzag up the hill, where is a natural crop of lavender in full bloom as far as we could see.

We crossed three drawbridges and entered the garrison;

the line walls were mounted with cannon and there are many outworks. On the shoulder of another hill stands a fort which commands this, and a third higher up, commands it in turn: at this place is the reservoir which supplies all the forts with good water and plenty of it. High above all this is a mortar battery. The place is said to be impregnable, but I think might be starved out very easily. Mount Genevre stands near, and although this was the longest day in June, is capped with snow.

As we entered the grand square we saw above 1,000 of our countrymen in a miserable condition, one half of them being nearly naked, with pieces of old blanket round them. A cold shudder came over me as I looked at them. Their condition was a disgrace to the French nation for there was abundance of clothing in the stores and since the month of March above 900 suits had been given to men who had entered the French service, which should have been served out to those prisoners who had been longest in garrison; and if a man entered prison to-day and volunteered tomorrow he got a new suit of prison clothing away with him.

There are good bomb proof barracks all round the square, which were used for the accommodation of prisoners. There we were taken and put into messes or sections 33 men in each, one man having charge; three of these sections formed a company, or unit, one man taking charge of the whole: he was called chief of a division and made out all returns for provisions, mess utensils, all sick reports, etc., and required to be a man that could speak French if possible. I got charge of a company and had many civilities shown me and was allowed more liberty than I would have had otherwise. Each gendarme had charge of five companies and all reports from them were made to the Marechal des Logis, who communicated with the Commandant.

Our provisions were scanty, consisting of 12 oz. of bread and 6 oz. of beef, with a very small allowance of rice or *callarances*, which were barely sufficient to support nature; we were allowed one *sou* and a half per day from the French, paid monthly and two *sous* per day from Lloyd's Committee. What bedding we had was rotten and full of vermin, from which we could not keep ourselves free. There was a market in the garrison where bread was to be got for three *sous* per lb., beef for six *sous* and wine for seven *sous* the bottle, brandy thirty-two *sous*. The people in the little villages in the valleys brought milk, meal, potatoes, etc., for sale, but money was very scarce.

We received a letter from Lord Beverley, with the welcome present of a franc a man: he resided as a prisoner at Moulins; he told us to be of good cheer as the exchange was going on.

On the 6th August there were eight men belonging to the 92nd regiment in this depot, John MacDonald and Alexander MacKinlay volunteered into the French service. I went to see if it was true and was nigh hooked myself. Captain Reilly said it was a glorious thing to serve an Emperor and offered to make me sergeant at once, never to be reduced without an order from the Emperor himself.

'Look at me,' said he; I enlisted a private soldier and see what I am now: an officer seldom springs from the ranks in the British service.'

I acknowledged the justness of his observation, but it had no effect on me I told him I was quite content to serve a King. The Captain did not trouble me again, but he certainly did not forget me for I often got a bottle of wine and a loaf of white bread more than the prison regulations warranted, which I have no doubt were sent by his order. I shook hands with MacDonald and had a glass of brandy with him; when I turned to go away he cried bitterly. He was made Corporal and in a few days marched for Landau, the headquarters of his regiment. Poor John was a good soldier but had his full share of bad luck. This left only six of the 92nd: James Sangster, James Gardner, John Semple, John Chambers, John Orr, and myself.

Letters concerning the exchange of prisoners were coming to the garrison from so many trustworthy gentlemen that nothing was talked of but Home Sweet Home. We were inspected by the General of the district, who seemed to take compassion on our ragged condition, he told us we would be provided with clothing before we went to England. The French are the best of promisers and seldom give you poor encouragement.

On the 24th of October, a letter arrived from Mr Anthony Aufrere, telling us that Mr MacKenzie the agent who had come from England to arrange about the exchange of prisoners had left the country without coming to any agreement. This was a grievous disappointment to us all. Some men cried like children, and others did not open their mouths to speak for days. I wrote to the Honourable Colonel Gordon at Lyons; he sent the men of our regiment three francs each: I also wrote to Sir John Hope, Colonel of our regiment.

A large party of the Rifle Brigade taken in a skirmish at Almeida arrived here, also a party of the 2nd battalion 4th regiment which had been shipwrecked in Cadiz Bay.

CHAPTER 5

The Strange Headquarters
of the 92nd

On the 5th November the snow, which we had seen at a distance began to come down and fell three feet the first night and continued until it was nine feet deep. This made us sit round the stoves; a kind of sulphury coal dust got among the hills was brought to us, this when slaked with water and wrought into balls made a strong fire. At length we got clothing served out, this made us look more respectable and our condition mended every day after this. About this time a body of men formed themselves into a *banditti*, stealing bread, money and everything they could lay their hands on; by dint of severe punishments we got them into order and kept them so. On 25th December, Christmas Day, a great many had something extra to eat and drink.

January 5th, 1811, Saturday, a dreadful cold day with wind and snow and pieces of ice flying about. We had to go to the town every fourth day for bread. This chanced to be one of the days for this duty and some men did not get the better of it for a long time. Our windows which were only oiled paper, were battered in by the storm. We made roads through the snow, and when the weather cleared up got out again, after being closely confined for a long time;

few people but those who have felt it can imagine what a winter is in the Alps. Our chief amusements were playing cards, dominoes, etc., and mending our clothes. On 16th January I wrote to Archibald Campbell, Esquire, our prize agent, for the first payment of our Denmark prize money.

An unlucky thing happened to me at this time: the best shirt I had was either stolen or blown over the line walls. I believe it was the former, for I had washed it that morning and was very particular in securing it. This was a great loss to me.

About the end of March we got rid of the snow after a long winter and I began my walks in the square from six to eight every morning weather permitting, then went in, took a little breakfast, and read or wrote till dinner was ready, then kept talking or hearing stories, news, etc., until afternoon when I walked for an hour in the square before we were locked up, which was always about sunset. This I carried on day after day.

Friday the 24th of May was a bright day for the six men of the 92nd regiment. We received our Danish prize money in answer to the letter I wrote to Mr Campbell, amounting to 53 Francs 10 *sous* each. This put us on a respectable footing; no doubt some of it was spent foolishly in drink, but much good was done also. Alexander Beattie of our regiment arrived; he had been detained in some hospital in the country since the retreat to Corunna. June 22nd, my 33rd birthday, was kept with great glee by the men of the regiment for the service I had done them in getting money.

On the 2nd October I received an answer to the letter I sent to Sir John Hope; it came from Alexander Bruce our army agent, with our pay from the date of my letter, at 3d per day, and we received 49 francs in a lump, and it was sent every month afterwards. This was an exceeding good change for the better, and we now enjoyed every comfort rational men could expect to be prisoners of war.

A party of the 89th regiment arrived. They had been taken at Malaga with their colonel, Lord Blaney, who did much good to the prisoners, in regulating the pay; he sent clothing for each man. This banished poverty, rags, and vermin from the depot. The charitable money was all given to the merchant seamen which bettered their condition also. All the waste ground about the garrison was converted into gardens and patches were sold or let out to the prisoners by the Marechal des Logis. I paid 60 *sous* for a piece and erected a kind of house with stones. This was called the headquarters of the 92nd regiment. And there I sat many an hour writing this narrative; at other times digging and planting or watering, but I never had a crop that came to maturity. So my French Lairdship brought me little profit but it was an employment to me and I had the pleasure of having a place to myself.

On 3rd October arrived a large party, taken in June, of the Guards, 42nd, 71st, 79th, 85th regiments and Johnston Caird of our regiment. From him we learned all the particulars of the army and of our own regiment, and all the news of the Walcheren expedition.

We passed this winter in a more agreeable manner than we did last. Christmas was kept in grand style, big loaves, sirloins of beef and plenty of wine and brandy etc. The jollification was kept up by some as long as they could raise the wind, and the new year came in with a great number of blue eyes and broken noses, and credit and money being gone things were at a dead stand until a fresh supply arrived.

One of the 71st regiment, Michael Floyd, brought between fifty and sixty doubloons into the garrison. Some plunder he had got his fingers over. He took the fever and was removed to the hospital, where the men in the ward with him, thinking he was going to make his exit took the money and divided it. But he recovered and an uproar was made about the Spanish gold. The men were put into close confinement and the money was delivered to the French authorities; they were afterwards sent to Gap and tried for robbery but were acquitted. What with law expenses and one thing and another Floyd did not get back half of his money.

This spring the crew of the *Alacrity* gun brig taken off the isle of Corsica was brought in here: each man received ten *sous* a day from the French for relieving some French prisoners confined by the Spaniards on a desolate island in the Mediterranean.

There came in about 200 soldiers, British, taken near Burgos, most of them belonging to the 3rd Buffs, 66th and 48th regiments. By what these men told us we thought the French were losing ground in Spain.

All the shoemakers and tailors were taken to Grenoble during the summer to work for the French.

On the 25th October there came in about 200 condemned prisoners from Bitch, many officers among them, who had been trying to escape, and had been guilty of other misdemeanours. They were closely confined having only two hours' liberty in the square every fourth day. They caused much trouble in the garrison and abridged our liberty much. A committee consisting of two French and two British was formed to do justice between man and man, concerning our rations and other affairs of the prison, the market, etc. Mr Nisbet the carpenter of the *Proserpine* frigate and Sergeant Lyle of the 21st regiment were chosen.

Christmas day and New Year's Day passed over much the same as the last, a battle royal was carried on until the French soldiers had to charge some of them into the barracks and all of us were locked up.

On Sunday 17th May 1812 I joined a society of Methodists who had hired a barrack room for a place of worship and prayer meeting. I continued with them until the breaking up of the depot, and received much edification: there might be about a hundred of us. In June we got new beds and blankets, things we had much need of. I was placed in a small barrack room with sixteen men and was very comfortable. There came in a party of the *Venerable*, 74, and some Royal Marine Artillery taken at Bilbao in Spain.

On the 25th November our regiment was put on the strength of Lord Blaney's Committee for pay, after our having received from an agent 3d. per day for 655 days and we received clothing from the committee for 1813. About this time a pawn broking company was formed and at Christmas many of our men had stripped themselves of every article of clothing they had and sold their pay for a month to come, at a discount. Orders came for 600 of the oldest prisoners to march; this caused a consternation and very long faces were made by the per cent gentlemen who had bought the payments beforehand.

On 27th January 1812, 200 marched for Arras; 200 next day for Valenciennes; James Sangster of our regiment marched with this division; 1st February, 200 for Givet; Alexander Beattie, 92nd went with this party. This gave us more room in the garrison.

We had much finer weather this winter than last. A new society called the Crusaders was formed among us by Sergeant-major Goldsmith, 23rd dragoons: a great many of the young men in the depot joined it.

On the 11th April I obtained liberty from Colonel D'Avrill, commandant of the garrison, to go into the country. With six others I went about from village to village eating white bread and drinking wine, for six days when our money was spent and we returned to the depot. A few days after this liberty was stopped because a party on leave had attempted to escape and were captured in Italy, not far from Turin, about 14 leagues from here. The Commandant said 'You British cry for liberty, but when you get it you do not know how to use it.' We all know the truth of this. And the Commandant was kind to us always as far as was consistent with the prison regulations.

On 24th May, an atrocious act was committed by one of the gendarmes, Perrier Houssier, when going his rounds. Some of our men were playing cards and had a light burning; without giving warning he fired through the door upon them and killed George Nail of the Rifles and broke the arm of Charles Reid, 3rd Guards. The Commandant declared his disapprobation of the cruel deed and caused a court to be held, half French, half British. The gendarme was sent to Grenoble to be tried by court-martial. He was condemned to slavery and our man was interred outside the walls very decently; prayers were read by Sergeant-major Goldsmith, 23rd Light Dragoons.

On 11th July there was a heavy fall of snow: this we were told was frequently the case after a mild winter. There came in a young lad of our regiment Alexander Murray who enlisted at Aberdeen only about seven months ago: he has certainly made the Grand Tour in extraordinary quick time.

The French kept all news from us as far as they could, concerning any defeat their armies had sustained. But it was impossible to hide altogether that they were nearly driven out of Spain and that things were not going on well in the north. 2nd November there fell 4 feet of snow, it then cleared up into frost.

16th November (1812), we heard of the burning of

Moscow and what great things the French had done in destroying the Russian armies. But on the 20th another tale was to be told: that the Austrians were entering Italy with a large army, and that the prisoners of war were to be sent off and the garrison to be put into a state of defence.

CHAPTER 6

The Journey Through France

I Marched on Wednesday the 8th December 1813, after being three years and five months a prisoner among the high Alps in this garrison: this is the longest time I have been in one place since I became a soldier. And no prisoner in France could have enjoyed better health than I did, or been more miserable when I entered it or more comfortable when I left it.

Some were sorry to have to march at this time of the year, and no doubt since we received a regular supply of money from Britain we were more comfortable here than we would have been with our regiments. For myself I was better prepared for the march now than at any time since I was a. prisoner, for 1 was strong and in good health, had two good suits of clothing, and ten dollars in my purse, which proved ten good friends to me during the winter.

The town and garrison were all in a bustle. Some of the merchants in town had trusted goods to a large amount to some of our people who acted as retailers for them, and got themselves swindled out of large sums of money. We were paid up to the 24th January 1814, by Lord Blaney's Committee. There were about 2,300 prisoners in the depot, and we were to march in five divisions.

We trudged along through the snow, every one with a light heart and a merry countenance, the inhabitants coming and shaking hands with us; they were sorry to part with us and no doubt we had spent much money among them. When far down the road I took a long look back at the garrison and thought it a dismal abode in the centre of the mountains among so much snow.

Some of our men got drunk on the road with brandy and one, Cochrane of the 42nd regiment, died through it and through being exposed to the cold. Came to St Crespin and were lodged in stables; the inhabitants brought us boiled beef, soups of all kinds, etc., wine for the ready penny, but all had to pay toll to the French guard before entering. 9th to Embrun. I bought a good blanket from one of our men for 26 *sous*; he thought it too heavy to carry but he repented doing so before he got out from the mountains. 10th to the village of Chorges. 11th Gap: we were inspected by the General of the Department. 12th, St Bonnet: a great fall of snow during the night; had to get guides to keep us on the road for rear of falling into the valley below, about half a mile down the side of a hill, in some places nearly perpendicular, to a place called Corff. 13th, to La Mure. The country is getting more level and the air is warmer, not so much snow lying. We were lodged in the theatre and had plenty of clean straw. 14th, a very wet dirty day; to Vif. With some others I went to an *auberge* and got lodgings for the night. We had supper and bed very comfortable. But this was a serious pull on my pocket, 5 francs each. After this, when I had to provide lodging as I sometimes had, I made a bargain with mine host before I took possession.

15th, Grenoble; we halted here on the 16th and 17th, were lodged in the barracks, but had the liberty of the town, which was not to the profit of some. 18th: we were now in a level country and a warmer climate: good roads. Came to

Moirans. 19th to La Cote St Andre. We were lodged nigh the church and could observe the good agreement between the Catholics and Protestants, one party having the use of the church in the forenoon and the other in the afternoon; they seemed to be on the best of terms with each other, a thing that is very rare. 20th to Bourgoin. 21st the shortest day but the longest march: seven country leagues or twenty-eight miles or more, into Lyons a large and populous city in a fine country and climate, well built, with broad level streets, squares, etc. Its lies in the cleft of two fine rivers. We crossed the river Rhone by a long stone bridge, well lighted with swinging lamps in the centre, which is the usual way of lighting streets in the principal towns of France. We arrived in front of the Hotel de Ville in the centre of the grand square and parted with the good old captain who had escorted us from Briancon and who had done all in his power to make us comfortable. We were closely confined in a large prison. 22nd, halted: we were visited by Colonel Hall of the 9th regiment, who paid us up till the 31st January 1814: this was the last money I received in the country.

On the 23rd we marched through the north-west part of the city; there are some fine streets by the side of the river on the quays, the houses ranging from five to six stories high. Crossed the Soane by a new stone bridge; many boats were passing up and down the rivers laden with the produce of the country. Saw the statue of a man standing on a rock; he had been a deliverer of the city in some war of ancient times. There was a great appearance of trade in Lyons and everybody seemed to be employed. We had a wet morning and a dirty road. Many fine, villages and chateaux lined the banks of the Soane, which we kept on our left most of the way to Villefranche: here we were at liberty to go where we pleased. Many of us got supper and a bed for 11 *sous*, but many never joined again. 24th, to Macon, a fine large town and a depot for Spanish officers, who were very inquisitive about the armies in Spain, but we had no news to give them of a later date than they had themselves. 25th, Christmas Day: many of our party got drunk and spent their all and the French commissary cheated us out of two days' pay; met a great many Spaniards changing their depot.

Came to Tournus, an ancient town in a fine country. It was very late before we got in after a long day's march and my wounded leg began to fail me and swelled much, owing to the long marches we were making every day. 26th to Chalons-sur-Soane, a fine town, good buildings and level streets, a market-place, and many boats on the river. I saw some corn mills here, built like large boats and anchored in the centre of the river: the millers do not require to draw water for their mills at this place. We crossed the Soane over a stone bridge into Isle St Laurens. There is a depot for conscripts here, and about 500 Spanish officers were in it. The Central Canal connects the rivers Soane and Loire at this place, which gives communication between the Atlantic and the Mediterranean. 27th, halted. 28th, to Beaune. We met many wounded French and Austrians: this let us know the fighting was not far off: 29th, to Dijon, the capital of the province of Burgundy. It seems to be well fortified with a ditch and line walls. In an open space in the shape of a horse shoe, stands the old palace, a noble building now getting out of repair; there are some fine churches and convents.

Into one of these large buildings we were bundled among 2,000 Austrians newly taken, and more arriving hourly. The nuns came among the wounded men and dressed their wounds. We were shifted to another part of the building and allowed port liberty. I took a walk round the ramparts, and a fine promenade they are for the citizens, with a full view of the country and the mountains of Switzerland. The town was full of troops and all seemed to be in a bustle, and wagons full of wounded French soldiers were arriving at intervals; we could hear guns firing at a great distance and were told it was at Besancon. 30th, halted.

It appeared to me that the men and women in the province of Burgundy were stouter and taller than I had seen anywhere else in France. The women at this time wore an odd kind of head-dress, a fine lace cap and a small black hat about the size of a tea saucer placed on one side of the head, tied under the chin with a black ribbon. 31st to Dijon, where we got billets.

CHAPTER 7

The Rascally Governor
of Maubeuge

Saturday, 1st January 1814, to Langres, a fortified town; it stands high and commands a view of the level country to a great distance. 2nd, to Chaumont which stands on a height and was seen long before we came to it; it is a depot for Spanish prisoners. 3rd, to Degary, a village; met a division of prisoners from Givet. 4th, to Joinville. This day I met forty-seven men of our regiment lately taken in the Pyrenees, got all the news from them that time would allow, as they were moving in another direction, 5th, to St Dizier: met a division of Spaniards on the march. 6th, to Vitry, an ancient town; many of the houses have their gables to the streets. We were crammed into stables by the side of the river Marne.

This day we passed four regiments of cavalry of the Imperial Guard, fine looking men, mounted on the best horses I have seen in the country. But we got the worst usage from them of any troops since we were prisoners. The roads were dirty and in passing they caused their horses to prance and bespatter us with mud, and we were in danger of being ridden over, while the troopers laid on us with their scabbards, cursing and calling us all the bad names they could think of. No doubt the men were grieved at being taken out of their comfortable quarters in Paris, for they did not seem to be troops that had seen much service, but we certainly expected better treatment from the Imperial Guard. Little did they think that in a few days afterwards many of them would be in the same condition as ourselves. A fine train of artillery accompanied them.

7th, to Chalons-sur-Marne, a clean town in a level unenclosed country; it is surrounded by a wall and a ditch. Got a gentleman's house to ourselves, with plenty of clean straw; good bread was sold in the marketplace, 6lb. for five *sous*. 8th, to Petit Logas, I was billeted on a farmer who used me very well.

As we advanced to the north we felt the weather colder, 9th, to the city of Rheims, which is walled in and has a deep ditch round it. There is a large cathedral with lofty spires, seen at a distance from the city. In it the kings of France were crowned. The buildings appear to be very old. At this time the town was full of French soldiers. We got some of our men into hospital here; they had been badly for many days and been conveyed in carts, but none of the towns we passed through would receive them. 10th, a heavy fall of snow during the night. This was a very cold day, wind north, in our faces. Passed more cavalry on the road who were more civil than the Imperial Guard.

Came to Craonne, which was full of troops; I was billeted in the country about a league from the town, 11th, to Laon. This town stands on a commanding height, and has a great appearance at a distance as you advance to it on a stone causeway with trees on each side of the road. It is strong by nature and art, and could easily be defended by a few brave men against a greatly superior force. There is a depot for artillery here and this day about forty or fifty pieces were taken off to the army, escorted by some troops of cavalry. There is also a large cathedral. 12th, halted: a cold frosty day. We were lodged in a church.

As some of a former division here had run off on the road to Dunkirk, and others had escaped into the Netherlands, the country was alarmed and we were escorted by a strong guard to Vervins, a long march and were put into close confinement at the end of it. 14th, to Avesnes: all these towns on the frontier are more or less fortified. 15th, came to the strong fortress of Maubeuge on the river Sambre which was to be our depot.

We crossed three drawbridges, as many line walls mounted with cannon, and ditches filled with water. Hundreds of people were working, putting the garrison into a state to be able to stand a siege, and as the authorities did not expect prisoners at this time we were lodged in good barracks, but no firing or utensils were given out and no rations but bread. An old blanket was served out to every three men, and every way was taken to annoy us.

Great stores of flour and all other kinds of provisions were brought in from the country. These articles were very cheap in the market and we could get a hatful of potatoes, apples or onions for one *sou*, and good beer or porter for four *sous* the quart, but money was very scarce among us.

For the first few days we had the liberty of the town, but when it was rumoured that a Prussian army was advancing the Governor ordered us to be put in divisions and work on the batteries. This we at once refused to do and some rash words spoken by some of our people enraged the Governor. It was given out that we were going to seize the town as some of our folk had been seen about the arsenal. The drums beat the alarm; the troops assembled under arms on the ramparts, and the National Guards in the streets, while a regiment of Lancers drew up in front of our barracks. We were all turned out and beaten and abused, and many a thump and blow was given us and many a *'diable'* and *'sacre foutras Anglais'* were bestowed on us. At last they drove us into the bomb-proofs under the ramparts and pointed two field- pieces to the only entrance, and here we were kept under ground for forty-eight hours, and for all this no reason was assigned: if the enemy had been within cannon shot we would have thought it all right. We got no provisions and water was scantily supplied through the stockade, a large gate. Many were very badly off but my comrade and I had just got a four lb. loaf at the time the scuffle commenced.

We got out on the 21st January, on condition that we were to make a palisade in front of our barracks and confine ourselves within it. We were now ready to promise anything or do anything to get out to the light of day once more and so we began the work. On the 24th an order arrived for all the prisoners to march. Next morning at daybreak we marched in a close body amounting to 1,800 men; we were strongly guarded. Snow and strong frost. Came after dark to Landrecies, a strongly fortified place. The French soldiers entered the garrison and we were quartered in some villages on the road to Cateau without anyone being left to look after us. On this long march my wounded leg began to fail and I was very lame for some days, yet I was contented and happy that I had made my escape from that rascally Governor of Maubeuge.

On the 26th we marched through the plains of Cateau to Cambray, a pretty large city with good streets and a large square; it is strongly fortified with a fort and citadel and other works and the country can be laid under water by the river Scheldt. In the citadel had been about 3,000 British prisoners; they had been marched off a few days before we arrived, and the French were busy mounting cannon there. Everyone seemed in a bustle and so many troops were marching in and out that we could not get bread until the evening of the next day. Many went without it, and some of the party began to steal bread, and got themselves and others beaten and abused by the French soldiers.

We got off at last and had to march on the 27th, 10 leagues to Peronne, a small strong town on the river Somme in the late province of Picardy. We got billets and were supplied with food by the inhabitants, and but for their kindness many of our party would have starved.

As we were too many to subsist together we separated into three divisions without the knowledge of the French; one took the road to Paris, and another made for the coast. I remained with the centre division. 28th, very bad road to Montdidier. 29th, Bolea, a little village. I was billeted on a fine motherly woman, who dried and mended my clothes. Poor woman, she had two sons in the *grande armee* who were I have no doubt, in a worse condition than I was.,30th, to Beauvais, a fine large town surrounded with hills on a small river. It has been a place of strength in days of yore and has some good buildings and streets, an ancient cathedral and a large marketplace. We were billeted in the country and were well used. 31st, halted and were mustered by the commissary; found our party numbered between six or seven hundred. We got bread and two francs each and were glad to get this trifle; it was a relief to many and was the means of keeping some from doing mischief among the country people, for some lawless gangs were making their appearance, although many desperadoes had left in the two divisions that went off without routes.

CHAPTER 8

Through Normandy

1st February, marched to Gisons, an ancient town in Normandy. 2nd, Vernon; crossed the river Seine over a long stone bridge; many boats were passing up and down the river. As this town was crowded with troops we were billeted in the country. 3rd, to Paucy. This day we went by a cross country road where, from some high grounds near, we had a view of Paris, with its domes and spires. It was about twelve o'clock and the sun was shining brilliantly upon them. We could trace the river Seine in all its turnings and windings up to the city. With some others I stood for more than an hour looking at a place we might not have an opportunity of seeing again. Others would not stir off the road to have a peep, but jogged on like donkeys, growling out, John Bull fashion, 'D— Paris and everything in it.'

4th, crossed the country to Evereux. All was in a bustle here: troops on the move, driving shot and shell; roads much cut up. 5th, passed a palace outside the town near the river, fine trees, ponds of water with fish swimming about: this place I was told formerly belonged to the Duke of Orleans. We crossed the country by a very dirty road; it rained all day; I was billeted at a village called Britty on a poor widow who, I believe, treated me better than she could well afford. 6th, to Cochen, a short march, the day being wet. 7th, to Verneuil, an ancient walled town; it being full of troops we were sent to the country. I was billeted on a jolly blacksmith who used me well. Observing a hole in my shoe he said he would mend it if I took it off. I did so, when for my comfort he spit upon it saying it was *bon pour la marche demain* for a prisoner of war, many a French soldier had not a shoe to his foot. 8th, on this day's march our party seized a wagon load of bread belonging to a party of Spaniards. They gave battle for it but were not able to withstand us. Some of our men had formed themselves into gangs, and let nothing pass them that could be lifted and we all got into trouble and disgrace through them. When we arrived at Montagne the Spaniards reported our party to the prefect of the department who called us a lawless *banditti*. He stopped our bread and money, called out the National Guard and gendarmes, and drove us all out of the town. I saw about fifty wolves' heads piled up at the gate of the Hotel de Ville all lately taken in time of snow. Wolves are plentiful in this wooded country, 9th, reached Bellesme.

10th February to Bonnetable, where I was billeted in a gentleman's house. When I told him I came from Edinburgh, he took me into a room to see his mother, a venerable looking old lady. When she learned where I came from she clapped her hands and called the household to see a man from the town where all the women went barefoot, for she had been there long ago when she was a little girl in the time of Prince Charlie. I was well entertained in this house.

Some villains of our party got us into trouble again by plundering; they were found out and lodged in jail to the good of us all.

11th to Le Mars where we halted on the 12th. This is a well built town with a cathedral and large square. There were about 700 British prisoners here from Givet. I envied them: they seemed very comfortable while we were doomed to wander about like vagabonds without a place of rest. 13th, marched on good roads with trees on each side, to Ecmoy where I had a good billet on a miller. Many of the inhabitants here live in caves hewn out of the solid rock. The weather had now changed for the better, warm, with sunshine. 14th, to Chateau du Loire very like an English town, with flying signs etc.: it is on the main road from Paris to Bordeaux.

On the 15th we reached Tours, where we thought our journey was to end and that we were to get into a depot at last. But no: this town was full of prisoners of all nations. We were joined by many of the men who left us at Peronne. We halted at some stables by the side of the river Loire at the end of a stone bridge by which you cross into the town which is large and well built, with broad level streets and a good looking cathedral. It stands on a plain in an elbow of the river, which is very broad here. We were waited upon by some of the committee for relieving British prisoners; they said their funds were done, but gave us six *sous* per man. A great number of young soldiers passed us in wagons on their way to Paris singing *'Vive, vive, Napolean le Grand.'* 16th halted. Although we had heard much of this Tours in Touraine, here we were not to remain, but were ordered to make for Rennes, the capital of Brittany.

We marched on the 17th, in company with Russians, Spaniards, etc. The road was quite covered with us until we came back to Chateau du Loire. I went to my old billet and was made welcome. The French seemed much more kind to the British than to any other prisoners travelling the country, bad as we might be at times. 18th, we left the main road and parted with our faithful allies. Came to Le Lude. 19th, to La Fleche. Here is a grand Military College and Hospital.

The people hereabout do not seem over attached to the present Government and some brigands had donned the White Cockade and taken a party escorting ammunition. They offered some of our men money to join them. I did not see any of them myself, or I should have gone with them if they would have accepted my company for I was weary of this vagrant life. 20th, to Sable. 21st, Melay, fine country billets. 23rd, Laval on the Mayenne a stirring town in the weaving business. It has two old castles. The inhabitants provided shoes for such of our men as were barefoot and were very kind to us. 24th, to Vitre, an ancient walled-in town; here we were all put into close confinement on account of some bad behaviour on the road.

We reached Rennes on the 25th and found our depot ready for us. It was an old nunnery and a very convenient place it was to be a prison. We were allowed at first to be out all day until many of our men were seen begging in the streets. These miscreants had their prison allowance and had no need except for drink. This caused the liberty to be withdrawn, with the consent of the chiefs of division and all decent men. A great number of prisoners were marched into this province; many of them were sent to Brest, but the British were never sent near the seaside. At this time the Austrian, Russian, Prussian, Spanish and British prisoners were said to be above 55,000 in this province alone. Yet provisions were plentiful and cheap, two lbs. of bread for three *sous*, beef five *sous* per lb., cider three *sous* per bottle; but money was very scarce.

The inhabitants were very charitable to many of our men and their goodness was often abused. Some men were taken about the coast trying to make their escape to England and were brought back; this caused us to be more strictly looked after.

Rennes is a fine large town well built, with good broad

streets, squares, etc. Our prison was on the north side of the town on the river Vilaine. About this time our rations were served out very irregularly and we began to suspect all was not right, and some of the military gentlemen looked rather dejected. We wrote to Lord Blaney for money, and signed for a month's pay we never received, for at this critical time any of the gentlemen of the committee who had money would not advance it.

On the 4th April, we were told by some gentlemen of the town, who communicated with us privately, that Paris was taken. On the 8th, one of our men belonging to the 51st regiment, got drunk, and while attempting to climb over the wall was shot through the body by one of the sentinels; he expired on the spot.

CHAPTER 9
The White Cockade!

On the 10th of April, Easter Sunday, an express came in, there was a great bustle in the town and about twelve gentlemen came opposite our prison, donned the White Cockade, pulled out white handkerchiefs and gave three cheers, which we answered by giving three times three. Our guard was immediately doubled; the military was called out and paraded the streets, and some gentlemen were stabbed and abused by the soldiers. From our top windows we could see what was going on on this side of the town. The quarters of the Commander-in-chief and Prefect of the Department were surrounded by the inhabitants clamouring for information. They were dismissed until 4 o'clock at which time the white flag was hoisted on the steeple of the townhouse amid shouts of *'Vive le Roi! Vive Louis 18!'* while our convent was not a minute behind. We hoisted a white sheet on a pole on the highest part of the building and three hearty cheers were given, while joy beamed on every man's face. The French soldiers were much dismayed. This great change was done in an orderly manner, all things considered.

The gentlemen of the town mounted all the guards and took possession of the Place des Armes. The soldiers were ordered to their barracks, except those that chose to hoist the White Cockade, which were very few indeed. Many of them went off and disbanded themselves. The cavalry and artillery took up a position on the other side of the river, opposite the town, and refused to submit until the Royalists sent them word that if they did not go to their barracks, or offered to fire a gun or cross the river, they would arm the British prisoners who would not be slow to attack them. This threat had the desired effect for during the night they withdrew to their former barracks.

In the evening some of our sailors climbed up the steeple of the townhouse and brought down the Imperial eagle, then cut down the Tree of Liberty that stood in the centre of the principal square (and a fine tree it was and had grown well since first planted) and burnt them there. The Royalists were in great triumph and kept patrolling the streets all night, and the military kept strong guard on their own barracks.

On the 11th, the Conscript Act and *Les Droits Reunis* were abolished by proclamation and beat of drum and all Imperial eagles and other coats of arms belonging to the old Government took flight. Twenty-one guns were fired when the proclamation of the Provisional Government was read. All the officers, civil and military attended, but I could see all this went down ill with the most of them.

We had now liberty to go anywhere we chose during the day, and in general we got home before dark by a kind of natural instinct.

On the 14th, orders were posted up printed in English and French stating that as the two countries were now at peace we were to behave to the inhabitants the same as if they were British, and any man guilty of crime was to be lodged in jail and sent prisoner to England; and as we were now at liberty we were to show ourselves worthy of it and behave like freemen; and we were to leave our prison and be billeted in the town. Signed by Count Conclaux, commanding for the French, and by Sir William Codrington, baronet, for the British. We gave three cheers on leaving the old convent, where we had been very well treated, but prisoners are never content. Routes were made out for the prisoners of different nations to leave. Three *sous* a league were given and a good many of the British, after getting their route and their money kept hanging about the town getting their names put down for other divisions, etc. About 1,200 British, lately taken, were encamped outside the town on the Champ de Mars. In this party was Sergeant-major Duncan MacPherson, who had been wounded. I spent a very pleasant day with him. He marched for Morlaix: this and St Malo were where - the British were to be embarked. I convoyed him on the road and assisted him with meat and money for which he promised great returns when we got to the regiment. I spent a few days very pleasantly and took long walks into the country. The military and the Royalists became more reconciled to each other and things began to have a more smooth appearance.

On the 27th April I marched with 200 men; we had a route, but I believe many came with us without one. Came to Ida. 28th, to St Pierre, and never men marched with lighter hearts some laughing and others singing, and *The Soldier's Return* was often sung with full chorus. 29th, St Maloes, and was very glad to see the salt water again. I had not seen it since I lost sight of the Mediterranean, 31st May. We marched to Fort Servan and got our names entered into the Commandant's books for embarkation. About 1,500 men were in the fort waiting for a passage. 150, the first on the books, went off in the evening in a French gun-brig, and some of our people made interest to get their passage in trading vessels. We looked out with great anxiety for vessels to take us away every tide. The barracks being choke full I sold my old friend my blanket and got a bed in town. Our rations here were one and a half pound of bread, one pound of beef and a pint of cider daily.

This place is strong by nature and art, being a rocky entrance into the bay, in which are several small islands mounted with heavy cannon. The town is surrounded by high walls and batteries and the sea nearly surrounds it at high water. A causeway defended by a strong castle connects it with the town of St Servan. There are some good buildings and shops and a fine quay for the shipping, and ships that have been lying idle for many years are being fitted out with all expedition. Some British vessels have come to this port already with goods and this place bids fair to be a brisk trading town. The dockyard for the navy, victualling offices, etc., are at St Servan; and a line of battleship and two frigates ready for sea are lying in an arm of the sea in rear of the town, where they have had a long rest.

On Tuesday, the 3rd of May the long looked for came at last. Five French gun-brigs arrived crowded with French from Plymouth. When they landed some of them got into a rage, showing us the bad loaves of bread they had got served out to them in England, and it was very abominable stuff. I had no way of parrying this, but by shaking my empty haversack and telling them I was leaving France with no bread at all. On this, a huge grenadier pushed his loaf to my face and said '*Pauvre diable*, take that and carry it back to England; I got it there yesterday.' I took it from his hand but did not eat it, as I never saw a worse compound. While I examined it I certainly thought many a man's case was worse than our own, and on summing up the matter I found I had little reason to complain of my treatment while a prisoner of war.

On the 4th we got on board and sailed. The wind set against us and all things went wrong with the French sailors; they brought the vessel to anchor off the Isle of Sark while the other brigs went off for England. Our tars offered the captain to take the vessel into Plymouth but of course this offer was rejected. 5th, got up anchor and made into Jersey.,The seamen were taken on board the guard ship and the soldiers landed at the pier where General Don and a brigade major received us. Many soldiers gathered round us asking questions about friends and comrades. Captain Corby of the 15th regiment with some non-commissioned officers took charge of this division, and we marched three miles to Groveville barracks on a fine sandy beach not far from Elizabeth Castle. Here we had an opportunity of bathing. We were inspected by a general doctor to see that we were clear and clean of scurvy and itch and other evils that come from France, and the whole party was reported free of any disease whatever. It seemed wonderful to some of the officers that so many men left to the bent of their own inclinations should be so free of disease. But it may be easily explained. Those men, being in the habit of marching every day in their divisions for months together, were more afraid of losing their party than if they had been with their regiments; while those who had been irregular in any way were not able to be among the first to reach the coast. And strange to many officers as it may appear I have seen nearly 1,000 men marching in France under charge of only two gendarmes and no more disorder among those men for weeks together, than I have seen in a regiment marching in Britain under the command of above 100 officers and non-commissioned officers, and these men generally in billets.

We received 1s 1d per day of pay, and got a shirt, shoes and a pair of stockings each. Bread sold at 4d per lb here; how different in France!

This island is strongly fortified all round the coast and the garrison consists of, General Don, Commander-in-chief, Major-General Horton, the 15th and 18th regiments at St Helier; a veteran battalion in the fort, and battalion 6th and 2nd battalion 66th. The able bodied men in the island form a militia and are drilled every Sunday.

On the 19th we marched at two o'clock in the morning for St Helier. I thought myself lucky in getting on board the gun brig *Intelligent*, but when we got to sea a French war vessel came bump upon us. This put us all into confusion. The French folks being so long out of practice do not know how to manage their ships. We were obliged to bear off for Guernsey and anchored off the town of St Pierre and reported our case to the Admiral. We asked to be put on board another vessel, but this was refused, so we set about putting things to rights and sailed on the 21st and anchored in Plymouth roads on the 22nd when the King's sailors went on board the *Salvador del Mundo* guard ship, formerly a Spanish 4-decker. The merchant sailors were sent into Plymouth, where they got £2 each to take them home, and the soldiers were landed at Mount Wise, and right happy were we all in getting our feet on British ground again.

We waited on the Green until the arrival of the Fort-major and other officers, when our names and regiments were taken down; we were marched to the district pay-master's office at Stonehouse, who gave us clothing to the value of £3. 1s. 6d. and we got our pay daily. We were formed into companies of sixty men each with officers and sergeants. Our division was commanded by Major T. Craigie of the Perth Militia, which regiment was doing duty at the Dockyard.

All the Germans and Maltese embarked for their own countries; the lame were sent to Chelsea where if I had been a friend to myself I should have gone. We got billets about four o'clock in the afternoon, and I was more tired hanging about this day than if I had marched thirty miles.

172

I was quartered near that infernal den called Castle Ray where every other door is a public house, full of sailors and soldiers, fiddlers and pipers, etc., so that the whole street stank of gin, tobacco, and red herrings.

I visited all the principal works about Plymouth, the Docks, Naval Hospital, Marine Barracks, etc. Nearly all the duty here is done by Militia regiments. All men landed with us whose regiments were in the district, which were the 11th, 20th, and 28th, joined them.

A riot broke out in the town concerning the bakers and millers mixing a white kind of pulverised clay among the flour and selling it to the public. The Mayor seized a ship-load of this stuff in the harbour consigned to some wealthy individuals of the town who had been carrying on this dia-bolical traffic for a long period. Some of them were lodged in the castle, the jail not being considered a safe place to keep them from the fury of the people.

The French prisoners were all cleared out from this, and the last division came from Dartmoor. On seeing us they ex-claimed against our country. But we easily convinced them that we had greater reason to complain for most of us came home in rags, while they were leaving Britain with new clothing and many of them with large sums of money.

I went to a fair at New Passage to see the Cornwall men wrestle with the Devonshire men for purses of money. Many a severe fall was given and some had to be carried out of the ring. Many coaches and gentlemen were here and I believe above half the women of both counties. The Cornishmen carried the day.

* * * * * *

The subsequent history of Daniel Nicol may be related in a few words. Having served continuously from 1794 to 1814, he, on the return of Napoleon from Elba, at once volunteered for service and joined a veteran battalion, until on the return of the troops from France, he was again discharged but was offered the rank of sergeant in his old regiment, then lying at Cork. This, however, he declined.

Exceptional interest attends the closing years of Nicol's life. In 1819 he was engaged by Robert Cadell, of the firm of Archibald Constable and Co., the publishers of Sir Walter Scott's novels, in whose publishing-house, he notes, on account of the extraordinary demand for Scott's writings, the work was often very heavy. When misfortune overtook the concern in January 1826, his services were retained by the trustees, and Mr Cadell invited him to remain, as, if he commenced business on his own account, he intended to engage him. Accordingly, in October of that year, when the stock was purchased by Cadell and Co., Nicol was at once employed. He continued in the same service till Mr Cadell's death in 1849, and his trustees subsequently employed him, till in May 1851 the business was purchased by Messrs Adam and Charles Black, to whom the rights of the publication of Scott's novels were transferred. In October 1851, however, Nicol died from inflammation of the lungs at the age of seventy- three, having spent twenty-two years in the army and thirty years in the service of Mr Cadell's firm.

Lightning Source UK Ltd.
Milton Keynes UK
UKOW02n1356081015

260104UK00002B/3/P

9 781846 772313